THE RISE OF AN

THE RISE OF ANALYTIC PHILOSOPHY

Edited by

Hans-Johann Glock

BLACKWELL
Publishers

Copyright © Blackwell Publishers Ltd 1997

ISBN 0 631 20086 X

First published 1997

Blackwell Publishers
108 Cowley Road, Oxford OX4 1JF, UK.
and
350 Main Street,
Malden, MA 02148, USA.

British Library Cataloguing in Publication Data

A catalogue record for this book is available from the
British Library.

Library of Congress Cataloging in Publication Data

Available from the publisher

Typeset by Cambrian Typesetters, Frimley, Surrey
Printed in Great Britain by Whitstable Litho, Kent
This book is printed on acid-free paper

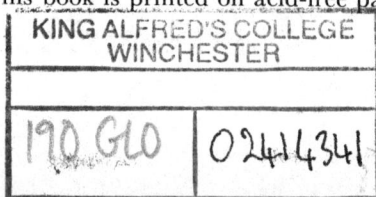

CONTENTS

Introduction   vii

1   Analytic Philosophy: What is it and why should one
    engage in it?   1
    Dagfin Føllesdal

2   Frege on Meaning   17
    Hans Sluga

3   Was Russell an Analytical Philosopher?   35
    Ray Monk

4   The Rise of Twentieth Century Analytic Philosophy   51
    P. M. S. Hacker

5   Why did Language matter to Analytic Philosophy?   77
    John Skorupski

Index   93

INTRODUCTION

Analytic philosophers have often prided themselves on the ahistorical nature of their philosophizing. Unlike traditional philosophy or continental philosophy, the story goes, analytic philosophy is a respectable science or skill; it uses specific techniques to tackle discrete problems with definite results, and hence need not seek refuge in discussing its own past. Ironically, from Russell and the Vienna Circle onwards, many analytic philosophers have at the same time been highly concerned with the origins of their movement, mainly in order to lay claim to the philosophical mantle of thinkers like Leibniz or the British empiricists. In recent years, the debate about the origins of analytical philosophy has been reopened by Dummett's claim that analytic philosophy is 'post-Fregean philosophy' and that it is based on the conviction that the philosophy of language is the foundation of the subject.

The contributions in this collection widen the scope of the debate beyond Frege, by taking into consideration the contributions of Russell, Wittgenstein and the Vienna Circle. They identify and assess some key ideas in twentieth century analytic phiosophy, in particular its concern with language. They also compare various definitions of analytical philosophy with the methodology and practice of eminent analytical philosophers. Although the contributors approach these topics from diverse angles, they seem to agree that one needs to distinguish between the birth of analytic philosophy on the one hand and the linguistic turn on the other, since otherwise paradigmatic analytic philosophers like Moore, Russell and perhaps even Frege himself would be excluded from the movement.

For Dummett, by contrast, the concern with language is the elusive factor X, long sought for in vain by Anglo-European conferences, which separates the phenomenological tradition on the continent founded by Husserl from Anglo-phone analytical philosophy, which he traces back to Frege. Dummett defines analytical philosophy as based on the idea that a philosophical understanding of thought *can* and *must* be given by an account of language. This contrasts with the philosophy of thought which retains the idea that philosophy should investigate thought, but claims that this investigation is independent of and antecedent to an understanding of language.[1] According to Dummett, this view informs not just phenomenology, but also recent work from within the Anglophone philosophical community; he mentions the Oxford philosophers Gareth Evans and Christopher Peacocke, but John Searle, Thomas Nagel and Colin McGinn also come to mind. Strictly speaking, therefore, these philosophers no longer count as analytic.

Dummett deserves credit for having revived the discussion about the origin of analytic philosophy. But even if one takes into account the scope of the canvas on which he paints, his brush-strokes are inaccurate. A concern with language does not mark off analytical from continental philosophy.[2] Paradigmatic analytic philosophers like Moore, Russell, Hart and Rawls would not accept that the basic task of philosophy is to analyse language. Equally, a work by Heidegger, Husserl's most famous pupil, bears the title *On the Way to Language*. And, for better or worse, Heidegger's followers have reached that destination. The idea that human experience is essentially linguistic is a commonplace among hermeneutical philosophers. Finally, the jargon of much continental philosophy is taken not from metaphysics or psychology, but from linguistics and semiotics.[3]

However, Dummett's definition of analytic philosophy is perhaps best understood not as an attempt to capture a historical phenomenon, but as a stipulation, its aim being to demarcate the kind of philosophy he regards as valuable. In this respect, Dummett is part of an established pattern. With the exception of some extremely biased treatments by Marxists and Popperians, discussions of the origin of analytic philosophy have by-and-large issued from philosophers who regarded themselves as members of the analytic tradition, and as proponents of analytic methods in philosophy. As a result, investigations into the origins of analytic

---

[1] *The Origins of Analytic Philosophy* (London: Duckworth, 1993), chs. 2, 12–3.

[2] A second problem with Dummett's definition of analytical philosophy is that he neither justifies nor explains the assumption behind it, namely that the fundamental task of philosophy is at any rate to analyse thought. My 'Philosophy, Thought and Language', in J. Preston (ed.), *Thought and Language* (Cambridge University Press: Cambridge, 1997), suggests that this startling idea is the result of two historical trends that came together in the *Tractatus*: the nineteenth century debate about the logical 'laws of thought' and the Kantian idea that philosophy, instead of thinking about reality, reflects on the way we think about reality.

[3] See e.g. H. G. Gadamer, *Philosophical Hermeneutics* (Berkeley: University of California Press, 1976), p. 19; J. Derrida, *Of Grammatology* (Baltimore: Johns Hopkins University Press, 1976).

philosophy have always been closely linked to the question 'What *is* analytic philosophy?', and that question in turn has often been linked to the question 'Why should one *do* analytic philosophy?'.

Dagfinn Føllesdal's paper 'Analytic Philosophy: What is it and why should one engage in it?' is concerned with precisely these two general questions, and for basically the same reason as Dummett, namely that Føllesdal is convinced of the superiority of analytic philosophy over the alternatives. But his conception of what these alternatives are, and hence of analytic philosophy, differs markedly from Dummett's. According to Føllesdal, analytic philosophy differs from various strands of continental philosophy such as phenomenology, Neo-Thomism, Neo-Kantianism or Neo-Marxism in that it cannot be defined by reference to particular doctrines, and from hermeneutics, which is essentially concerned with understanding and interpretation, in that it cannot be defined by reference to particular problems. Nor can it be defined by reference to a method, such as conceptual or linguistic analysis, since prominent analytic philosophers such as Quine do not fit that bill. Føllesdal also rejects the attempt to define analytic philosophy *genetically*, as a tradition of philosophers who argue with each other and go back to the same historical roots, since Bolzano, who is in many respects an analytic philosopher, did not actually influence the rise of analytic philosophy.

Føllesdal's own definition of analytic philosophy is 'that analytic philosophy is very strongly concerned with argument and justification', with the reasons there are for accepting or rejecting a philosophical position. He counters the objection that some analytic philosophers, such as Wittgenstein, showed no such special interest, by insisting on a broad conception of what is to count as 'argument' and 'justification'. Moreover, he is prepared to bite the bullet of accepting that, according to his definition, it 'is almost a tautology' that all 'truly great philosophers are analytic philosophers'. It is wrong to regard analytic philosophy as one trend among others. The analytic/non-analytic distinction *runs across* other divisions. Phenomenologists, existentialists, hermeneutics, Thomists, etc., are *more* or *less* analytic, depending on the weight they attach to rational argument. And because of this central concern, analytic philosophy is not just '*good* philosophy', but also a force in support of dialogue and tolerance.

By contrast to Føllesdal, Hans Sluga, in his essay 'Frege on Meaning', approaches analytic philosophy not so much as a cause to be praised (or condemned), but from a more detached historical perspective. For Sluga, analytic philosophy is neither defined by reference to a preoccupation with language, nor as the herald of reason, but as 'a field of overlapping and diverging discourses'. Sluga is interested not just in the historical roots of Gottlob Frege's own semantic ideas, but also in the roots of our present-day preoccupation with this aspect of Frege's work, at the expense of others. Sluga contradicts this semantic perspective by claiming that Frege is a philosopher of language 'only in a derivative sense'. There is 'a hierarchy of concerns in Frege which proceeds systematically and historically from mathematics, through epistemology, to the design of the syntax of a formalized language, and from there finally to questions of meaning.' According to Sluga, semantical ideas are largely absent from *Begriffsschrift*; their gradual emergence is significantly influenced by the South-West German branch of Neo-Kantianism, and ultimately fuelled by Frege's evolving ideas about mathematics. Frege was forced to modify his original doctrine of judgments because of problems over the status of identity statements. In *Begriffsschrift*, such statements are treated as synthetic. This became a problem after the attempt to prove the existence of self-subsistent logical objects in *Grundlagen der Arithmetik* forced Frege to introduce the notion of a value-range, and with it the ill-fated Axiom V, according to which for every concept there exists a class having for its member precisely those objects that fall under the concept.

For Frege, Axiom V is an identity statement, but as one of the axioms of his logicist system, it better not be synthetic. This threat was averted by the sense/meaning distinction. While identity statements in which the two expressions have the same meaning yet different senses are synthetic, identity statements in which the two expressions have the same sense are analytic. Axiom V is analytic by these lights, but foundered on Russell's paradox. As a result of this depressing discovery, the semantical ideas which had previously been mere tools of the logicist programme took on an independent interest for Frege. Finally, the fact that Carnap and Wittgenstein came to know Frege during his final, 'semantic', period explains why he came to be seen as primarily a theorist of meaning, in spite of the fact that he regarded such a theory as impossible, and in spite of his abiding concern with attacking the empiricist conception of mathematics.

Ray Monk's paper 'Was Russell an Analytical Philosopher?' takes its provocative title from Dummett's aforementioned definition of analytic philosophy. According to Dummett, analytic philosophy is based on three tenets: the goal of philosophy is the analysis of *thought*, the study of thought is to be sharply distinguished from the study of the psychological process of *thinking*, and the proper method of analysing thought is the analysis of *language*. Monk aims to show that, according to this definition, even Bertrand Russell would fail to count as an analytic philosopher. This would certainly amount to a *reductio ad absurdum* of Dummett's characterisation of the analytical tradition, since even he regards Russell as one of the founders of that tradition.

Monk goes on to show that Russell, throughout his many transformations, held on to the conviction that philosophy should be occupied not with language, but with the world and our knowledge of it. It was only in 1918 that Russell came to develop an explicit interest in language. This was the result of accepting Wittgenstein's radical suggestion in the *Tractatus* that logic and mathematics are essentially linguistic. But, far from taking this to indicate the linguistic nature of philosophy, Russell concluded that logic and mathematics are not essential to the truly philosophical quest of establishing the nature of reality. Moreover, while before 1918 Russell subscribed to the anti-psychologism commended by Dummett, he afterwards re-psychologized both logic and linguistic meaning: 'far from accepting that the only proper method of analysing thought was the analysis of language, he would have maintained, on the contrary, that the only proper way of analysing language was to investigate thought, that the theory of meaning is a branch of psychology'.

What makes Russell an analytic philosopher, according to Monk, is not the linguistic turn, and not even primarily his rejection of idealism, but his rejection of his own early Hegelian monism in favour of an atomistic conception of reality. And this revolution was fuelled not so much by Moore, but by developments concerning the foundations of mathematics (Weierstrass, Dedekind and Cantor). Russell became convinced that the royal road to philosophical insight lies not in synthesis or system building, but in the analysis of propositions into their constituent parts, a process which he never regarded as essentially linguistic. Consequently, Monk proposes to define analytic philosophy not by reference to the linguistic turn, but in a much more straightforward way, namely by reference to the method or programme of analysis.

In 'The Rise of Twentieth Century Analytic Philosophy', Peter Hacker follows a similar line. Hacker distinguishes sharply between the emergence of analytic philosophy and the linguistic turn. Yet, he also insists that the twentieth century is, philosophic-ally speaking, the age of language and logic, and that the task of exploring these themes fell to analytic philosophy. According to Hacker, however, the main force behind this linguistic turn was Wittgenstein rather than Frege. Hacker recognizes that, in a loose sense, the bulk of philosophy is analytic. But, unlike Føllesdal, he regards such a loose notion as fruitless, and proposes to treat twentieth century analytic philosophy as a historical trend, albeit a multi-faceted one which underwent many changes.

The starting-point of this tradition is the venerable idea of analysis, of decomposition into constituents. What distinguishes modern analytic philosophy from the ham-fisted mental analysis of the British empiricists is its anti-psychologistic orientation. The result of this transformation is the 'first phase' of modern analytic philosophy, namely Russell's programme of logical analysis and Moore's programme of conceptual analysis. Hacker points out that neither Russell nor Moore regarded their enterprise as linguistic; yet he also maintains that Russell's theory of description creates some pressure towards conceiving analysis not as the identification of extra-linguistic entities, but as an intra-linguistic operation of sentential paraphrase.

At the same time, Russell, like Frege, conceived of the instrument of logical analysis, the logical calculus they had invented, as an *ideal language* which replaces ordinary language for the purposes of science and philosophy, because it alone is guided by the essentially non-linguistic structure of thought. It was against this background that Wittgenstein's *Tractatus* inaugurated the linguistic turn, and thereby the 'second phase' of analytic philosophy. The central features of this revolution were: firstly, the idea that logical analysis does not construct an ideal language, but discovers the logical form which any possible language must already possess underneath its grammatical surface; secondly, the claim that the propositions of logic are tautologies rather than description of some kind of reality; thirdly, the slogan that philosophy is a 'critique of language' which sets limits to the linguistic expression of thoughts. These ideas moulded the 'third phase' of analytic philosophy, namely Cambridge analysis between the wars and the logical positivism of the Vienna Circle, and thereby shaped important aspects of both British and North American philosophy in the second half of the century.

By contrast to the other papers, John Skorupski's 'Why did Language matter to Analytic Philosophy?' focuses neither on historical issues nor on the question of how best to define analytic philosophy. Instead, it provides a critical account of one of the central features of twentieth-century analytic philosophy, namely its preoccupation with matters of language and meaning. Language mattered to analytic philosophy because rules of language-use came to be seen as the primitive phenomenon in terms of which meaning, thought and the a priori could be understood. According to Skorupski, this 'priority thesis', and the connected idea that the use of a term exhausts its meaning, were in turn inspired by two even more fundamental ideas, namely that all assertoric content is factual and that no fact is intrinsically normative.

Skorupski tries to undermine both the priority thesis and the idea that meaning is use, but without lapsing into the Platonist view that concepts and propositions are abstract entities. He thinks that the later Wittgenstein has succeeded in showing that no object can have intrinsic meaning. At the same time, however, this 'no-intrinsic-meaning argument' leaves open a third alternative, according to which concepts are neither abstract nor language-relative. Indeed, Wittgenstein's own reflections on what it is to apply a rule can be used to show (against some of Wittgenstein's remarks) that the dichotomy between facts and rules is untenable. There must be normative contents which are neither factual nor expressions of language-rules. On this account, concepts are neither abstract entities (as Platonism holds) nor reflections of linguistic conventions (as the analytic tradition has it), but constituted by non-linguistic norms of a cognitive or epistemic kind, norms with which linguistic rules have to dovetail. The resulting view rejects analytic philosophy's conception of meaning and the 'a priori'; but, Skorupski assures us, it can still retain its deflationary view of metaphysics as based on 'pseudo-problems'.

The basis for this collection was a one-day conference held in April 1995 at the University of Reading. The speakers at the conference were Hans Sluga, Ray Monk, Peter Hacker and John Skorupski. The articles by Sluga, Monk and Hacker are versions of the papers they gave on that occasion. Skorupski's article deals with a topic related to the one he discussed in his presentation at the conference, while the paper by Dagfinn Føllesdal was contributed subsequently. The conference was supported by a travel grant from the British Academy and by a conference grant from the Mind Association, for both of which we are very grateful.

Whether or not analytic philosophy and good philosophy are one and the same thing, the essays in this collection show that analytic philosophers are capable of dealing with their own tradition in a way that combines argumentative vigour with diligent scholarship and a good sense for the important strands of history.

Hans-Johann Glock

Department of Philosophy
The University of Reading
Reading RG6 6AA
England

I

ANALYTIC PHILOSOPHY: WHAT IS IT AND WHY SHOULD ONE ENGAGE IN IT?

Dagfinn Føllesdal

In surveys of contemporary philosophy, it is customary to distinguish two main currents: the analytic and the continental. Analytic philosophy is then in turn divided into two principal traditions: one inspired by logic, of which Bolzano, Frege and Russell are the early main protagonists, and one oriented towards ordinary language, in which G. E. Moore, the later Wittgenstein and J. L. Austin played a central part. Continental philosophy, by contrast, comprises trends such as phenomenology, existentialism, hermeneutics, structuralism, deconstructivism, neo-Thomism, neo-Kantianism, neo-Marxism, as well as assorted other 'neo-isms':

ANALYTIC PHILOSOPHY		CONTINENTAL PHILOSOPHY						
logical	ordinary language	pheno- menology	existent- ialism	hermen- eutics	structural- ism	decon- struct- ivism	neo- Thomism	neo- Marxism

Analytic philosophy has dominated in the English-speaking world for the last sixty years and is now encroaching upon the continent. This distresses some, who regard analytic philosophy as anathema, as a turning away from serious philosophy. Others greet it as a happy development; they regard analytic philosophy as something positive. Just as there are societies and journals for phenomenology, existentialism and other varieties of continental philosophy, there have during the last decade been established societies and journals for analytic philosophy, such as *Ratio*.

Yet, when we ask 'What is analytic philosophy?' it is not easy to find an answer. Like most labels, it is highly malleable and can be molded to different purposes, in particular the following two:

(1) *Polemics*. Label polemics is rather widespread, because it is so easy: First one defines a label in such a way that it stands for a view that it is easy to refute. In the best cases, one is able to find somebody who actually has this view. However, the more stupid the view, the less evidence is supplied that anyone actually has it. This is, however, a minor matter compared to the next step: one

now applies the label to a large number of philosophers, too many to discuss individually, and then writes them off as a group. In many cases the whole first step is skipped: one just applies the label to a large group of philosophers without bothering with definition, texts or interpretation.

Such polemics are, unfortunately, widespread, especially in popular discussions of philosophy. They close people's minds and they tend to illustrate the adage: What one is not up on, one is down on. To avoid this, evaluation, positive as well as negative, should always be based upon careful interpretation.

(2) *Surveys.* In surveys one usually arranges the items to be surveyed into suitable groups according to the features one happens to be interested in. The grouping may facilitate one's grasp of the field and the groups are normally given labels. This is a relatively innocent use of labels. However, as soon as one turns to evaluation or criticism, the objections mentioned under point (1) apply: all evaluation, in particular criticism, should be based on careful interpretation.

One main point of my paper will be that the label 'analytic philosophy' is inappropriate even for survey purposes, that the whole division of contemporary philosophy into 'continental' and 'analytic' is fundamentally flawed. The questions I want to raise are these: What is the philosophy we call analytic? Why should one engage in this kind of philosophy? And how does it compare with other major currents of contemporary philosophy – is it antagonistic or conciliatory towards them, are they compatible or incompatible?

The flaws of the classification of contemporary philosophical trends are not unlike the flaws of the following classification in a 'certain Chinese encyclopedia' which has been reported by Jorge Louis Borges, and which you may have encountered in Foucault's writings:

animals are divided into: a) animals belonging to the Emperor, b) embalmed, c) tame, d) sucking pigs, e) sirens, f) fabulous, g) stray dogs, h) included in the present classification, i) frenzied, j) innumerable, k) drawn with a very fine camel hair brush, l) *et cetera*, m) having just broken the water pitcher, n) that from a long way off look like flies.[1]

[1] Jorge Luis Borges, 'Die analytische Sprache John Wilkins' ', in Borges, *Das Eine und die Vielen. Essays zur Literatur* (München 1966, p. 212). Quoted by Michel Foucault in *The Order of Things* (New York: Random House, 1970), p. xv.

The problem with this Chinese encyclopedia is: there is no principle of classification, or so it appears at least to people from our cultural background. The classification of *philosophical* currents suffers from *two* problems. Firstly, there is no principle of classification. Secondly, it is unclear what the different traditions are that are supposed to be classified – how can they be defined or at least roughly characterized? This problem is particularly pronounced with respect to our topic – analytic philosophy. What *is* it?

Conceptual analysis

One customary way of defining 'analytic philosophy' is by appeal to its method: it is said to be based on conceptual analysis. This fits in with some early characterizations of its method. As early as 1905, Moore spoke of the 'analysis of philosophical concepts', and in his *Our Knowledge of the External World* of 1914 Russell writes of the 'logico-analytic method', without, however, saying much about the peculiarities of this method. Friedrich Waismann, in his article 'What is logical analysis', which appeared in the last issue of the journal *Erkenntnis* before the war, writes that 'philosophy can be called the logical analysis of our thoughts'. According to Waismann, this analysis consists in 'dissection of a thought into its ultimate logical elements . . . as the chemist analyses a substance'.[2]

This comparison may well be apt with respect to G. E. Moore, who, for example, attempted to dissect the concept 'horse' in the same way in which a horse can be dissected anatomically.[3] But Waismann's characterization fits only a minority of contemporary analytic philosophers. What of Quine, for example, who denies that there is such a thing as concepts? Is it not beyond doubt that he is an analytic philosopher? Some of the early proponents of analytic philosophy may have thought of themselves as performing conceptual analysis. However, only a few of those who nowadays are classified as analytic philosophers can be characterized as analysts of concepts, meaning or language. We have here a choice: Either we may restrict the label 'analytic philosophy' to these few philosophers and stop applying it to those many philosophers who are classified as analytic philosophers in surveys of contemporary philosophy. Or we may try to define 'analytic philosophy' in

---

[2] *Erkenntnis* 8 (1939–40), pp. 265–289. English translation in Friedrich Waismann, *Philosophical Papers* (Dordrecht: Reidel, 1977), pp. 81–103.

[3] G. E. Moore, *Principia Ethica* (Cambridge: C.U.P., 1989; 1. ed. 1903), pp. 7–8.

such a way that it fits the great variety of philosophers who are normally called 'analytic'. In this article I shall do the latter.

Doctrines, Problems, Approaches

Some philosophical currents, such as phenomenology, are determined by their perspectives or doctrines. A phenomenologist is someone who has distinctive views about intentionality and other related topics. Neo-Thomists, neo-Kantians, neo-Marxists, etc., are equally characterized by their views. This does not hold, however, for hermeneutics, which is defined rather by its range of problems. Hermeneutics is concerned with questions of understanding, and with the interpretation of texts and other manifestations of the human mind, to speak with Dilthey. It only engages the many other problems of philosophy in so far as the latter are connected with understanding and interpretation. But as regards their views, the various proponents of hermeneutics differ sharply.

Even at this stage, therefore, it is apparent that the standard classification of the main currents of contemporary philosophy conflates two distinct principles of classification: doctrines and problems. Furthermore, the tradition with which we are concerned, analytic philosophy, cannot even be characterized by reference to either doctrines or problems. Analytical philosophers discuss a variety of philosophical problems, and they hold utterly different views about these problems. I know of no philosophical view which is shared by all or even most analytic philosophers, at least not of a view which is not completely trivial. In my view, what distinguishes analytic philosophy is rather a particular way of *approaching* philosophical problems, although, as we have seen, this approach must not be identified with a specific method of analyzing philosophical concepts. But in what does this distinctive approach consists? This is the question that will occupy us now, and it is not an easy one.

Genetic affiliation: schools

But before we turn to this question, let us first note that by now we have encountered three different principles of classification: according to *doctrines*, according to *problems*, and according to *ways of approaching* them. We jump from the one to the next and to the third, as in the Chinese encyclopedia, and without a unifying principle of classification. For any classification, this is a serious difficulty. Hence, before attempting to characterize analytic philosophy, we should consider an alternative principle of classification, which may have occurred to you already: perhaps the classification of currents of philosophy should be regarded as a genetic classification, a classification of philosophical *traditions*, of *schools of philosophers*, of philosophers who are teachers and pupils, engage in debate with one another, and go back to the same philosophical roots.

This classification works well with some major currents: phenomenology, neo-Thomism and other 'neo-isms'. Yet it does not work so well for hermeneutics. In antiquity, the Middle Ages and in early modern philosophy, one already finds hermeneutic endeavors. These endeavors were often undertaken in isolation, and without knowledge of one another. Nevertheless, they have in common that they have contributed to a philosophical understanding of the topic of understanding and interpretation. Similarly for existentialism, where one finds early existentialist outsiders such as Augustine.

There have been attempts to bring analytic philosophy within the ambits of such a genetic scheme of philosophical schools. For example, it is often claimed that analytic philosophy began with Frege and Russell (the logical branch) and G. E. Moore (the ordinary language branch). It has even been claimed that 1903 can be regarded as the year of birth of analytic philosophy, because of the simultaneous publication of Russell's *Principles of Mathematics* and Moore's 'Refutation of Idealism'. But this claim is not entirely serious. It will be easily granted that more than twenty years earlier, Frege already engaged in analytical philosophy. However, Frege does not create problems for the genetic classification of philosophical trends. After all, his writings were thoroughly studied by Russell, and in *Principia Mathematica* Russell and Whitehead write that 'in all questions of logical analysis, our chief debt is to Frege'.[4] All that is required to include Frege among the analytic philosophers is to shift its date of birth from 1903 to 1879, the year in which *Begriffsschrift* was published.

Nevertheless, the conception of the main currents of philosophy as philosophical schools is unsatisfactory. I have already mentioned the problems in the case of hermeneutics and existentialism. In these cases, philosophers are grouped together not because they are

---

[4] Alfred North Whitehead and Bertrand Russell, *Principia Mathematica* (Cambridge: C.U.P., 2d ed., 1925–27 (1. ed. 1910)), p. viii.

teachers and pupils, but because they tackle the same problems. In my view, analytic philosophy creates even more serious problems than hermeneutics and existentialism for the view that the main currents of philosophy consist of schools of thought. Take as an example Bernard Bolzano.

In my view, Bolzano, born in 1781, was an outstanding analytic philosopher. Early in the nineteenth century he anticipated many central ideas of Frege, Carnap, Tarski, Quine and others, and tackled them in an exemplary fashion. It is with good reason, therefore, that Anders Wedberg starts the last volume of his history of philosophy, the presentation of contemporary philosophy, with a chapter on Bolzano.[5] Then follow Frege, Russell, Moore, and the other philosophers of our century. To say that Bolzano is an analytic philosopher cannot mean that Frege, Russell, Moore and other analytic philosophers are *pupils* of Bolzano. Frege does not mention Bolzano, and seems not to have known of him at all. It is not improbable that some of Bolzano's impulses reached him via intermediaries. But to back the genetic thesis that Bolzano exerted a decisive influence on Frege, one would have to believe in the migration of souls: Frege was born in 1848, the year of Bolzano's death (however, Bolzano died six weeks after Frege's birth).

It appears that Russell did not know of Bolzano either, in spite of the fact that Bolzano dealt at length not only with the philosophy of logic and the philosophy of language, but also with other topics on which Russell worked, such as the philosophy of Leibniz. Bolzano remained generally unknown until the work of Heinrich Scholz, of Kaila in Finland and of Wedberg and his pupils. Until recently, for example, there was no entry on Bolzano in the *Encyclopedia Britannica*. Only Husserl paid attention to Bolzano; he explicitly thanks him in *Logische Untersuchungen* as well as in other works. If the main currents of philosophy are schools, for which teacher/pupil relations and actual influence are decisive, Bolzano must be regarded as a phenomenologist. However, in his work one encounters very little of the views about intentionality and related themes that characterize phenomenology. Instead, all those who have studied Bolzano have concluded that he is a typical analytic philosopher. 'Great grandfather of analytic philosophy' Dummett called him, thereby claiming only a systematic connection, not a genetic one.[6]

---

[5] Anders Wedberg, *A History of Philosophy*, Vol. 3: From Bolzano to Wittgenstein (Oxford: Clarendon Press, 1984; Swedish ed. 1966).

[6] Michael Dummett, *The Roots of Analytic Philosophy* (London; Duckworth, 1993), p. 171.

For this reason we are well advised to abandon the idea that the classification of philosophical currents is a genetic classification of philosophical schools. This may hold true of neo-Thomism, neo-Kantianism, neo-Marxism, etc., but hardly of any other currents. Some currents, such as phenomenology, are characterized by certain views or theses, others, like hermeneutics, by a particular range of problems. What we have here is a mixture of diverse criteria, but no common basis of classification, a situation similar to that of the Chinese encyclopedia.

But analytic philosophy continues to demand our attention. We have not yet established what it is. We have a few negative answers: analytic philosophy is not a school, one can be an analytic philosopher without having studied other analytic philosophers, and without in turn influencing other analytic philosophers. Moreover, there is no philosophical view or method of conceptual analysis which is shared by all or most analytic philosophers. But what can we say *positively* about analytic philosophy? I have already mentioned that analytic philosophy appears to be characterized by its way of approaching philosophical problems. The question is therefore: what characterizes this approach?

I have alreay remarked that there are many analytic philosophers, such as Quine, who do not fit the view of analytic philosophy as a kind of conceptual analysis. It is true that analytic philosophers like to investigate language. But philosophy of language is only part of analytic philosophy. Analytic philosophers can be found in all areas of philosophy, for example in epistemology, ethics, aesthetics, philosophy of mind and metaphysics. Moral philosophers like Rawls only rarcly pronounce on language and the philosophy of language; and yet they are analytic philosophers.

Argument and justification

The answer to our question is, I believe, that analytic philosophy is very strongly concerned with argument and justification. An analytic philosopher who presents and assesses a philosophical position asks: what *reasons* are there for accepting or rejecting this position? This question necessitates an investigation of what follows from the position at issue, and from what other positions it can be derived. How can one strengthen or invalidate this position? This is what is usually meant when one asks: what precisely does this position mean? One then discovers that minute differences in the way a position is formulated determine whether it is acceptable or not.

This, I believe, is one reason why analytic philosophers are so often concerned with analyzing language. Linguistic analysis is necessary to avoid ambiguities and unclarities which may be crucial to the validity of a line of argument.

To be sure, there are analytic philosophers who claim that successful linguistic or conceptual analysis is the only aim of philosophy. G. E. Moore was of this opinion, as was Wittgenstein, early as well as late. In philosophers who have been influenced by Moore and Wittgenstein, one often encounters this idea. Thus Schlick writes in his well-known essay 'The Turning Point in Philosophy', which introduced the first volume of the journal *Erkenntnis*:

> By means of philosophy statements are explained, by means of science they are verified. The latter is concerned with the truth of statements, the former with what they actually mean.[7]

The same contrast between science and philosophy is also evident in Waismann's aforementioned essay 'What is logical Analysis?':

> . . . philosophy and science express two very different types of attitude of the human mind. The scientific mind searches for knowledge, i.e. for propositions which are true, which agree with reality. On a high level, it rises to the construction of a theory which connects the scattered and in their isolation unintelligible facts and in this way explains them. . . . Now, what can be gained through philosophy is an increase in inner clarity. The results of philosophical reflection are not propositions but the clarification of propositions.[8]

By contrast, other analytic philosophers, indeed a majority, hold that philosophy is concerned with truth. Many of them also believe that it resembles science. Thus, in the twenties Russell wrote that philosophy is 'essentially one with science, differing from the special sciences merely by the generality of its problems.'[9] Similar views are to be found from Mach to Quine.

---

[7] 'The Turning Point in Philosophy', in A. J. Ayer (ed.), *Logical Positivism* (New York: Free Press, 1959), p. 56. German original 'Die Wende der Philosophie', *Erkenntnis* 1 (1930/31).

[8] *Loc. cit.*, p. 81.

[9] *Sceptical Essays* (New York: Norton, 1928), pp. 69–70.

In the same vein, Frege writes that his attempts to clarify language do not constitute his real aim. He never believed that philosophical problems could be solved through the analysis of language, but only that such analysis can help us to understand the problems better. He certainly would not have shared Wittgenstein's view that linguistic analysis provides the solution to philosophical problems, as is maintained in the Preface of the *Tractatus*, or that the root of the problems lies in language, as we read in several places in *Philosophical Investigations*.

This provides a good illustration of my contention that analytic philosophy cannot be identified by reference to a collection of shared theses. Even in response to a fundamental question like 'What is philosophy?', analytic philosophers provide totally different answers. Nevertheless, no one can seriously doubt that these philosophers – Moore, Wittgenstein, Schlick, Waismann, Russell and Frege, and analytic philosophers.

For this reason the emphasis on argument and justification seems to me more characteristic of analytic philosophy than a concern with conceptual analysis, which forms only a part of it. My thesis, that analytic philosophy is not characterized by specific doctrines or problems but by argument and justification can easily be checked. To refute it, one need only find philosophers whom we regard as analytic, but who care little about argument and justification.

Wittgenstein

Wittgenstein and his followers immediately come to mind. Do we find arguments and justification by these philosophers? Or are they perhaps not analytic philosophers after all? Von Wright, an outstanding analytic philosophers, has intimated the latter, and he writes of Wittgenstein's later philosophy 'that its spirit is alien and even hostile to the typically "analytic" approach'.[10]

It is not surprising, therefore, that the late Russell regarded the influence of Wittgenstein on the subsequent development of philosophy as a misfortune. In a review of J. O. Urmson's book *Philosophical Analysis: Its Development Between the two World Wars* Russell expressed his aversion as follows:

[10] Georg Henrik von Wright, 'Analytic Philosophy: a Historico-Critical Survey'. Reprinted in von Wright's *The Tree of Knowledge and Other Essays* (Leiden Brill, 1993) p. 32.

The later Wittgenstein . . . seems to have grown tired of serious thinking and to have invented a doctrine which would make such an activity unnecessary. I do not for one moment believe that the doctrine which has these lazy consequences is true. I realize, however, that I have an overpoweringly strong bias against it, for, if it is true, philosophy is, at best, a slight help to lexicographers and at worst, an idle tea-table amusement.[11]

What is argument and justification?

For reasons that I will discuss later, I regard argument and justification as very important elements of philosophical activity, and, where they are absent, I become skeptical. However, I have a broad conception of what to count as 'argument' and 'justification'.

As we all know, in philosophy, as in other areas, argument means more than just deductive argument. The theory of deductive argument is very well developed, and familiarity with deductive argument is important for understanding and applying other types of argument. The types of argument which we encounter in philosophy and other areas are usually variants of non-monotonic arguments, that is, arguments in which adding new premises may cast doubt on a conclusion that would follow without these premises.

Philosophy also consists of intricate descriptions of emotions and of human attitudes and activities such as perception. Here we are eager to find forms of description and distinctions which suit the material, while at the same time creating clearness and cohesion. Clearness and cohesion are key concepts in philosophy. Perhaps even more than in the special sciences, philosophy desires to see 'how all one common weft contrives, each in the other works and thrives' ('wie alles sich zum Ganzen webt, eins in dem andern wirkt und lebt').[12]

In philosophy, as in other sciences, it is necessary to alternate between the investigation of general connections and details. The theory of the general connections must fit the details, and the details must find a place in the more general theory. It is through this kind of 'reflective equilibrium' that we arrive at justifications of our philosophical insights, of the general insights as well as of the detailed, specific ones. Goodman, Israel Scheffler and Rawls have

---

[11] From the reprint in Bertrand Russell, *My Philosophical Development* (New York: Simon and Schuster, 1959), pp. 216–7.
[12] Goethe, *Faust* I, verse 447 ff.

introduced this idea into the contemporary debate. The question of what sound argument and valid justification amount to is itself a question within analytic philosophy. Moreover, it is an important one, which can be answered in diverse ways.

At the beginning of our century, Husserl had already proposed a conception of justification similar to that of Goodman, Scheffler and Rawls. He writes that the unity that ties together the various statements of a treatise or theory confers an 'interrelated validity' on these statements.[13] Husserl also emphasizes that the 'manifold prelogical validities act as ground for the logical ones'.[14] What I find particularly interesting in Husserl is that he, even more than Goodman, Scheffler and Rawls, reflected on the question of why this kind of connection confers validity. In his view, the reason is that the 'opinions' (*Auffassungen*) on which we ultimately rely are not thematized by us, and in most cases never will be. Each claim to validity and truth is founded on this *life-world* of non-thematized opinions which we have never made the subject of any judgment.

One might think that this only makes matters worse. Not only do we rely on something uncertain, but on something which we never thought of, and which, consequently, we have never subjected to conscious scrutiny. Husserl maintains, however, that it is precisely the non-thematized nature of one's opinions which makes them the last court of justification. In his view, 'accepting' and 'believing' are not attitudes which we adopt on the basis of deliberate decisions. What we accept, and the notion of accepting itself, are part of our life-world; and, according to Husserl, there is no possibility of escaping this never thematized acceptance. I quote: 'It is impossible to evade the issue here through a preoccupation with aporia and argumentation nourished by Kant or Hegel, Aristotle or Thomas.'[15]

I regard this idea of Husserl's as a stimulating contribution to our contemporary discussion about ultimate justification and the theory of reflective equilibrium. Reflective equilibrium comes closest to what I have called argument and justification in my discussion of analytic philosophy. This idea provides us with a conception of analytic philosophy that is open without being vacuous. The great heroes of analytic philosophy, such as Bolzano,

---

[13] Edmund Husserl, *Erste Philosophie*, 3. Vorl. Husserliana VII, 19. 33.

[14] *Die Krisis der Europäischen Wissenschaften und die Transzendentale Phänomenologie*, §34, Husserliana VI, 127.15–16.

[15] *Loc. cit.*, 134, 35–37, David Carr's translation.

Frege and Russell, fit well into this picture. Through the great weight which they have given to argument they have contributed to the philosophical enterprise insights into several general connections, as well as detailed studies and distinctions. Yet, Moore and Wittgenstein have also made important contributions. They give little insight into general connections, but they have given descriptions and drawn distinctions; moreover, they have detected difficulties to which all attempts to provide a systematic philosophy must be alive. Detecting difficulties is also an important contribution to philosophy, indeed, a very important one.

Non-analytic philosophers

My characterization of analytic philosophy through the concepts 'argument' and 'justification' might appear to be too open and wide. Are there any philosophers which do not count as analytic by these lights? To take twentieth century philosophers as examples, I think that my characterization does not fit Heidegger and Derrida. Instead of arguments and justification, they predominantly make use of rhetoric; one finds in their work many of the traditional rhetorical devices. Thus Husserl wrote in his copy of *Being* and *Time*: 'What is said there is my own doctrine, but without its deeper justification'.[16]

Similarly for Derrida. Typical in this respect is his 'discussion' with Searle. Searle defends himself against Derrida's critique of his position on the grounds that he has been misunderstood and misquoted. Instead of discussing these objections, Derrida takes to addressing Searle as SARL (Societé anonyme de responsibilité limitée), to indicate that Searle is not willing to take responsibility for his positions. The audience applauded Derrida, but this is not analytic philosophy.

This is by no means to say that Heidegger, and perhaps even Derrida, could not provide philosophical insights. But to uncover these insights it would be necessary to formulate their respective views in a clear manner, in order to find out what can be adduced for or against them. The lack of argument and justification poses a peculiar problem to such a reconstruction. Argument and justification contribute to the clarification of what is claims; where they are absent, interpretation becomes difficult.

---

[16] Husserl's copy of *Being and Time*, p. 62.

Hermeneutics and analytic philosophy

In his excellent article 'Analytic Philosophy: a Historico-Critical Survey', with which I am largely in agreement, von Wright has contended that *hermeneutics* is incompatible with analytic philosophy.[17] I, for my part, am of a quite different persuasion. Von Wright offers two main reasons for his thesis. *Firstly*, hermeneutics emphasizes the difference between social sciences and humanities on the one hand, and natural sciences on the other. Emphasizing this difference is at odds with the thesis of the unity of science. *Secondly*, according to von Wright, those analytic philosophers who have concerned themselves with questions of interpretation and understanding, for example Quine, Sellars and Davidson, are naturalists, while hermeneutics strives to conceive of human beings as *historical* and *cultural*.

The problem with von Wright's two reasons is that both analytic philosophers and proponents of hermeneutics have advocated very diverse opinions. Not all analytic philosophers propound the thesis of the unity of science. Much depends on how this unity is to be understood. Nobody holds that the social sciences and humanities conduct experiments of the kind common in natural science. Only a few hold that the social sciences and humanities are dealing with exceptionless covering laws like the natural sciences. Even in the natural sciences, the idea of such laws has almost died out, and with it the *nomological*-deductive method. By contrast, some of us mean something completely different by the *hypothetico*-deductive method: the hypotheses need not have the status of laws, but rather of assumptions, which must be tested through their connections with other statements in the network of an overall theory.

As an example of an analytic approach to hermeneutics I will mention Wolfgang Stegmüller's article 'The So-Called Circle of Understanding'.[18] This essay, as well as contributions by other analytic philosophers, constitute what I call *analytic* hermeneutics.

As regards von Wright's second reason for his thesis that hermeneutics and analytic philosophy are incompatible, namely

[17] Von Wright, *Op. cit.*
[18] Wolfgang Stegmüller, 'Der sogenannte Zirkel des Verstehens', in K. Hübner and A. Menne, eds., *Natur und Geschichte* (Proceedings of the 10th German Congress for Philosophy held in Kiel, 8–12 October 1972), Hamburg 1973, pp. 21–45. English translation in Wolfgang Stegmüller, *Collected Papers on Epistemology, Philosophy of Science and History of Philosophy*, Vol II, Synthese Library, Vol. 91 (Reidel: Dordrecht, 1977).

that hermeneutics is non-naturalistic, I only want to observe the following: Firstly, the naturalism of Quine, Sellars and Davidson is shared only by *some* analytic philosophers, indeed, probably only by a minority. Secondly, it is by no means obvious that hermeneutics is incompatible with naturalism. We are dealing here with a difficult philosophical problem that calls for careful argumentation. Quine and Davidson both contend, albeit on different grounds, that understanding and interpretation can be accounted for naturalistically. Incidentally, Davidson's efforts in this respect have aroused a certain interest among literary critics, as witnessed by the recently published *Literary Theory after Davidson*.[19] It appears to me that literary theorists are at preent looking for philosophical foundations of their theories. Derrida offered something to them, which some literary theorists found attractive, while analytic philosophers have hitherto offered very little in this respect. Here lies an important challenge to us analytic philosophers.

Conclusion

One conclusion that we can draw from my reflections in this essay is that analytic philosophy cannot be defined by reference to specific philosophical *views* or *problems*, or through a specific *method* of conceptual analysis. Instead, what distinguishes it is a particular *way of approaching* philosophical problems, in which arguments and justification play a decisive role. Only in this respect does analytic philosophy differ from other 'trends' in philosophy.

The traditional classification of contemporary philosophy, with analytic philosophy as one trend among others, is therefore misleading. It would be better to say that the analytic/non-analytic distinction runs *across* other divisions. One can be an analytic philo-sopher *and·also* a phenomenologist, existentialist, hermeneuticist, Thomist, etc. Whether one is an analytic philosopher depends on what importance one ascribes to argument and jutification. There are, for example, phenomenologists who are *more* analytic, and others who are *less*. In the same vein, we can classify philosophers from all eras of the subject's history. Thus Thomas Aquinas is one of the most analytical Thomists. And Aristotle, Descartes, as well as a large number of other truly great philosophers are analytic philosophers. The way I have defined analytic philosophy, this is almost a tautology for me.

---

[19] Ed. R. W. Dasenbrock (Pennsylvania: Pennsylvania State University Press, 1993).

We therefore have to revise our classification of contemporary philosophy into the following:

	pheno-men-ology	exist-ent-ialism	herm-eneu-tics	struc-tural-ism	decon-struct-ivism	neo-Thom-ism	neo-Marx-ism	ethics	natur-alism	. . . etc . . .
MORE ANALYTIC ↑	Hus-serl									
		Hei-degger								
↓ LESS ANALYTIC										

We still have two principles of classification at work here, according to doctrine (phenomenology, existentialism, naturalism, etc.) and according to problems (hermeneutics, ethics). The groups are not exclusive, one may, for example, be both a phenomenologist and an ethicist. And within each group one will have those who are more analytic and those who are less.

Let me draw one final conclusion. We should engage in analytic philosophy not just because it is *good* philosophy, but also for reasons of individual and social ethics.

When we try to bring our fellow human beings to adopt our own points of view, we should not do so either through coercion or through rhetorical devices. Instead, we should try to induce others to either accept or reject our point of view on the basis of their *own* reflections. This can only be achieved through rational argument, in which the other person is recognized as an autonomous and rational creature.

This is important not just as regards individual ethics but also as regards social ethics. In our philosophical writing and teaching we should emphasize the decisive role that must be played by argument and justification. This will make life more difficult for political leaders and fanatics who spread messages which do not stand up to critical scrutiny, but which nevertheless often have the capacity to seduce the masses into intolerance and violence. Rational argument and rational dialogue are of the utmost importance for a well-functioning democracy. To educate people in these activities is perhaps the most important task of analytic philosophy.

Department of Philosophy,
University of Oslo
PO Box 1020
Blindern
0315 Oslo 3
Norway

Translated from the original German by H. J. Glock

II

FREGE ON MEANING

Hans Sluga

I

We look today at Frege as one of the founding fathers of analytic philosophy and tend to forget that the general respect in which he is held now in philosophy is of relatively recent origin. It is true that Russell drew attention to him fairly early on. His discussion of Frege in appendix A of *The Principles of Mathematics* (1903) spawned, however, no extended interest in his work. Its one important effect was to alert Wittgenstein to Frege, but the dissemination of Wittgenstein's own thought and the recognition of Frege's decisive role in it took again several decades. Then there were Husserl, Carnap and a few other independent thinkers who responded in one way or other to Frege's work in the first decades of the century. For all that, it was really only in the period after the Second World War, more than a century after his birth and more than a quarter century after his death, that Frege came into his own.

This belated recognition influenced, of course, how we then came to think of him. The historical constellations into which Frege grew up, the philosophical and mathematical debates of the second half of the nineteenth century, had long passed and even the philosophical tradition which we now call analytic philosophy had by then undergone a number of significant transformations.[1] It had

[1] Following common practice, I take analytic philosophy here as originating in the work of Frege, Russell, Moore, and Wittgenstein, as encompassing the logical empiricism of the Vienna Circle, English ordinary language philosophy of the post-war period, American mainstream philosophy of recent decades, as well as their worldwide affiliates and descendents. This is hardly a precise characterization, and it is by no means unproblematic. Both wider and narrower characterizations have been offered. On some accounts, Plato and Aristotle were analytic philosophers, on others not even Gareth Evans – who might be considered a paradigm of the type – turns out to belong to the analytic tradition. I believe that a plausible case can be made for the understanding of the term 'analytic philosophy' I have adopted.

This is not to deny the possibility that future historians of philosophy might adopt quite different classifications. In a discussion of French structuralism Michel Foucault once dismissed it as a phenomenon of small consequence, saying: 'Instead it seems interesting to me to study formal thinking, the different types of formalism, which have traversed Western culture during all of the twentieth century . . . I'm thinking of the unusual skill of formalism in painting, the formal research in music, the significance of formalism in the analysis of folklore, the segas, architecture, the sagas, the application of some of its forms to theoretical

come to see itself as being chiefly a philosophy of language, its central concern being a theory of meaning. What was more natural at this point than that analytically minded thinkers should look at Frege primarily from that perspective? That they should treat him as primarily a philosopher of language and that they should pay so much attention to his doctrine of sense and reference? Not only was the essay On 'Sense and Reference' the first text of Frege's to be translated into English, it also became his most often reproduced and most widely read piece of writing.[2] It is certain that Wittgenstein and Carnap contributed much to this picture of Frege as a theoretician of meaning. For it seems to have been Wittgenstein who suggested the collection of the essays edited by Black and Geach which focuses so exclusively on questions of meaning. And Carnap's *Meaning and Necessity* (1947) also contributed importantly to this image. The picture of Frege that emerged in this way in the late forties and early fifties was elaborated by men like Max Black, Peter Geach, Aonzo Church, Gustav Bergmann, and J. L. Austin, and has received its canonical expression more recently in the writings of Michael Dummett.[3]

It is for all that a misleading picture, one that fails to acknowledge how radically the discursive context of analytic philosophy has shifted since the time of Frege. It treats the concerns of the analytic tradition as more or less permanent and as

---

thinking.' Twentieth century formalism, he said, 'is in my opinion as significant as Romanticism or Positivism in the 19th century.' ('How Much Does it Cost for Reason to Tell the Truth', in *Foucault Live*, ed. Sylvère Lotringer (New York: Semiotexte, 1989), p. 233. From such a perspective, certain portions of 'analytic philosophy', and certainly all of Frege's work, might be considered part of the evolution of twentieth century formalism, whereas other portions (such as Oxford ordinary language philosophy) would lie more or less outside it.

Given the broad current consensus on the meaning of the term, the question arises when philosophers first came to think of analytic philosophy as a single, coherent movement. The answer is surely that this happened only in the period after the Second World War, that is, roughly at the same time when Frege's current reputation was established. This gives one reasons to think that the two events were probably not unconnected.

[2] Max Black published an English translation of the essay in 1948 in *Philosophical Review*, vol. 57, and Herbert Feigl another one a year later in H. Feigl and W. Sellars, *Readings in Philosophical Analysis*. The former was eventually incorporated in Max Black's and Peter Geach's *Translations from the Philosophical Writings of Gottlob Frege* (1952) and reprinted with further modifications in later editions. J. L. Austin's translation of *The Foundations of Arithmetic* appeared in 1950.

[3] It is worth recalling that Dummett considers both Wittgenstein and Carnap important influences on his conception of analytic philosophy and of his understanding of Frege's place in the analytic tradition. See 'Can Analytic Philosophy be Systematic and Ought it to Be?' in Michael Dummett, *Truth and Other Enigmas* (Cambridge/Mass: Harvard University Press, 1978).

identifiable in terms of our current preoccupations, when the tradition has, in fact, undergone a series of discursive breaks, from an early concern with the foundations of mathematics through an emphasis on empirical science to its present focus on language and meaning. Even this is too simple a picture, since each of the authoritative figures of early analytic philosophy – Frege, Moore and Russell, Wittgenstein, Schlick, Carnap, and Neurath among them – brought into the tradition his own very specific and personal agenda. Analytic philosophy, far from being the monolith as which it has occasionally been described, was from the beginning the result of complex negotiations between a number of very different discursive possibilities.[4] It makes for that reasons little sense to claim, as Michael Dummett has done in his most recent book, *Origins of Analytic Philosophy*, that the analytic tradition is distinguished by a coherent set of beliefs, still less that it has its own axioms, as he also says.[5] Like any other philosophical tradition it is, in reality, a field of overlapping and diverging discourses.

We get a sense of Frege's own motivations from the first pages of his *Foundations of Arithmetic* where he identified two major concerns: a mathematical and an epistemological one.[6] With respect to the former, he said that his primary goal was to return mathematics to 'the old Euclidian standards of rigor,' (p. 1) a project which in his eyes demanded, among other things, a more rigorous conception of proof in analysis and sharper definitions of 'the concepts of function, of continuity, of limit and of infinity.' (*ibid.*) He added to this the need for a precise definition of the concept of number and of the natural numbers which he singled out as the foundations of the whole of arithmetic. He concluded that 'we shall hardly succeed in finally clearing up negative numbers, or fractional or complex

---

[4] I have tried to describe some of these intersections of different discursive concerns in early analytic philosophy in 'Grösse und Grenzen der analytischen Philosophie', in Friedrich Stadler, Hg., *Bausteine wissenschaftlicher Weltauffassung*, Veröffentlichungen des Instituts Wiener Kreis vol. 5 (Vienna-New York: Springer, 1996).

[5] Michael Dummett, *Origins of Analytic Philosophy* (Cambridge/Mass.: Harvard University Press, 1994), pp. 4 and 11.

[6] Readings of Frege certainly differ in the weight they attach to this passage. While many interpreters, myself included, take it to be programmatic of Frege's work as a whole, others, those who see Frege primarily as a philosopher of language, will generally downplay its significance. In support of the former reading it can be said that the sentiments expressed in these first pages of *The Foundations of Arithmetic* correspond to remarks in the preface to the *Begriffschrift* as well as to the summary of his scientific achievements which Frege wrote for Ludwig Darmstaedter in 1919. In quoting from *The Foundations of Arithmetic* I rely in the following on Austin's translation.

numbers, so long as our insight into the foundation of the whole structure of arithmetic is defective.' (p. ii)[7]

These mathematical considerations he augmented with philosophical ones. 'Philosophical motives too have prompted me to enquiries of this kind,' he wrote. (p. 3) Those enquiries were to determine that arithmetical truths are analytic, that they are derivable from purely logical principles, and that the principles of geometry are synthetic a priori truths. While he felt free to diverge from Kant where necessary, he drew attention 'to the extent of my agreement with him, which far exceeds any disagreement.' (p. 101) Kant, he insisted, did great service in distinguishing between synthetic and analytic judgments, he was also right in characterizing geometrical truths as synthetic a priori, he was, in fact, 'a genius to whom we must all look up with grateful awe.' (*ibid.*)[8] The grounds for his admiration are not difficult to locate. Like Kant, and like the neo-Kantian philosophers who were his contemporaries, Frege saw himself as the opponent of a fashionable empiricism and psychologism. Hence, he expressed the fear that his conclusions would be disliked most by 'those empiricists who recognize induction as the sole original process of inference (and even that as a process not actually of inference but of habituation.)' (p. xi) At the same time he expressed hope that one or the other of them would 'take the opportunity to examine afresh the principles of his theory of knowledge.' (*ibid.*)

Such remarks were clearly aimed at John Stuart Mill and his German admirers. Mill appears, in fact, throughout *The Foundations of Arithmetic* as Frege's most formidable opponent, his *Logic* being one of the most often cited texts. While he did not deny Mill a 'spark of sound sense', Frege complained that it 'is no sooner lit than extinguished, thanks to his preconception that all knowledge is empirical.' (p. 9) This radical empiricism was the more worrying, since Mill's *Logic* had been enthusiastically received in Germany by empirically, naturalistically, and psychologistically

---

[7] It seems to me evident that the title of Frege's book is meant to refer to the natural numbers as the foundations of arithmetic, not to foundations in general. In emphasizing the mathematical side of Frege's work I find myself in agreement with Paul Benacerraf's 'Frege: The Last Logicist' in Peter French, et al, (eds.), *Midwest Studies in Philosophy VI*, (Minneapolis: University of Minneapolis Press, 1981), reprinted in Hans Sluga (ed.), *The Philosophy of Frege*, vol. 2 (New York and London: Garland, 1993). I do believe, however, that Benacerraf offers us a one-sided picture of Frege, a picture that needs to be balanced in the way I suggest here.

[8] I find no evidence in Frege's text for the claim, advanced by some interpreters, that these words of praise were not genuinely meant.

inclined philosophers and scientists. Justus Liebig, the charismatic founder of organic chemistry, and Hermann von Helmholtz, the physicist, physiologist, and philosopher of science, were among its devotees.[9]

In *The Foundations of Arithmetic* we see Frege, thus, poised between two discursive possibilities, one internal to the mathematics of his time, the other central to the problem situation in contemporary philosophy. He was, indeed, not the only one pulled in these two discursive directions. Such a dual focus was, in fact, characteristic of much work done by mathematicians in the Göttingen tradition initiated by Gauss. Frege, who had obtained his own Ph.D. in Göttingen, was thus no isolated figure; his agenda was rather very much that of the local discursive context. What distinguished him, however, from others working in that context is that he set out to bridge the gap between mathematical and philosophical concerns through the invention of a new logical language, the calculus of his *Begriffsschrift*. This move was motivated, so it seems, by his acquaintance with Leibniz and his work on the logical calculus. The story of how Frege came to be engaged in these matters still remains to be told, but it is worth noting here that during the middle of the nineteenth century, i.e. a generation before Frege, a renewed interest in Leibniz had awakened in Germany which had led first to Erdmann's edition of Leibniz's philosophical writings to be followed soon by Gerhardt's more extensive edition of both the philosophical and the mathematical works.[10]

One peculiarity of Leibniz's work on the calculus bears crucially on the question of the evolution of Frege's concern with questions of meaning. For Leibniz had occupied himself intensively with the construction of an appropriate system of *signs*, but had not elaborated on the semantic features of the calculi he designed. The same is, in fact, also true of the early Frege. He, too, devotes great care to the syntax of his formal language and to the axiomatic structure of his system of logic. His discussion of the semantic features of this calculus is, on the other hand, almost casual and takes up relatively little space. What is more, his assumptions in this area are, to begin

---

[9] When Frege was writing *The Foundations of Arithmetic*, there existed, in fact, already two German translations of Mill's work. Schiel's translation, from which Frege quoted, had been published in 1862–63 and was by then in its fourth edition, the other, by Theodor Gomperz, published in 1872–73, was in its second edition.

[10] Frege was certainly familiar with the Erdmann edition. He had also read Adolf Trendelenburg's important essay on Leibniz's characteristic language, as is evident from the preface of the *Begriffsschrift*.

with, largely traditional; he borrows his language and his ideas from the philosophical literature of his own time. Since questions of meaning are not his major concern in the early period, he freely quotes terms and theories that are in general currency.

This is evident in the *Begriffsschrift* where he first lays out his new logic. The major achievement of that work is indubitably the precise formulation of an axiomatic, bivalent propositional calculus and of a first-order quantificational calculus. It does not, on the other hand, contain a precisely conceived account of meaning. There is, in particular, no theory of truth or anything equivalent to be found in it. Anyone familiar with Frege's later development or with the evolution of the analytic theory of meaning will find it surprising that the concepts of truth and falsity are wholly absent from the book. In describing what we would call truth-functional connectives, Frege speaks only of propositions being affirmed or denied, not of their being true or false. When he subsequently tries to justify the construction of symbolism, he borrows his ideas about meaning largely from Trendelenburg. Following Trendelenburg's comments on Leibniz's calculus, Frege puts a striking emphasis on the signs themselves. He writes emphatically: 'Let no one despise symbols! A great deal depends upon choosing them properly.' And to this he adds: 'We need a system of symbols from which every ambiguity is banned, which has a strict logical form from which the content cannot escape.' The idea seems to be that in a properly constructed symbolism meaning will take care of itself.[11]

Despite some efforts to clarify these matters, it was only five years later, in *The Foundations of Arithmetic*, that Frege expressed a sustained interest in questions of meaning; and it was only in the 1890s', some thirteen yars after the publication of the *Begriffsschrift*, that he came up with the sense-reference distinction. I conclude then that there exists a hierarchy of concerns in Frege's thinking which proceeds systematically and historically from mathematics, through epistemology, to the design of the syntax of a formalized language, and from there finally to questions of meaning. Frege can, thus, be called a theorist of meaning and philosopher of language only in a derivative sense.[12]

---

[11] 'On the Scientific Justification of a Begriffsschrift,' in Gottlob Frege, *Conceptual Notation and Related Articles*, tr: and ed. by Terrell Ward Bynum (Oxford: Oxford University Press, 1971), pp. 84 and 86.

[12] Wolfgang Carl's illuminating book *Frege's Theory of Sense and Reference* (Cambridge: Cambridge University Press, 1994), rightly emphasizes the epistemological side of Frege's thinking, but it seems to me to separate unduly his mathematical concerns from his interest in semantics. The result is a somewhat disjointed picture of Frege's thought.

II

To trace Frege's descent into semantics requires us to go back to the *Begriffsschrift*. He begins the exposition of his new logic there with an account of the nature of judgment whose subsequent modification will prove a central motivation for the later sense-reference semantics. The crucial point of the early doctrine is a distinction between the content of a judgment, which may or may not be asserted, and the judgment itself. Even so, Frege offers us only a rudimentary account of the distinction he considers so fundamental. He calls the 'judgeable content', for instance, a 'mere combination of ideas' (*Vorstellungsverbindung*) and the judgment 'the affirmation' of such a content, but he explains neither what an idea nor what a combination of ideas is, and he has nothing further to say about what affirmations and denials are. Only one thing matters to him in this discussion: that he can now single out the conceptual content of the judgment as that which is significant for logic. This has, among other things, the consequence for him that he can set aside all modal considerations from his logic. Asserting that the modalities of possibility and necessity affect only the force with which a judgeable content is affirmed, he has given himself grounds for ignoring questions of modality as not genuinely logical at all. 'By saying that a proposition is necessary I give a hint about the grounds of my judgment,' he writes, and then with added emphasis: 'But, since this does not affect the conceptual content of the judgement, the form of the apodictic judgment has no significance for us.' (p. 13)[13]

Frege's words should recall a passage from Kant's *Critique of Pure Reason* similarly concerned with modal judgments. According to Kant:

> The *modality* of judgments is a quite peculiar function. Its distinguishing characteristic is that it contributes nothing to the content of the judgement . . . but concerns only the value of the copula in relation to thought in general. (B 100)

Nor is Kant the only name to mention in this context. For Kant's idea had been revived and elaborated by a number of philosophical

---

[13] Frege claimed shortly later that the distinction between judgeable content and judgment was all his own, that he was 'making it in contrast to common practice.' The remark is, however, misleading, since the distinction was widely discussed in the logical literature of Frege's time.

authors in Frege's time. Thus, Christoph Sigwart introduces his *Logic* of 1873 with a distinction between 'the living act of thinking' performed when we make an actual judgment and the ideas to which the act is directed. Unlike Frege, he assumes, however, that the separate ideas that enter a judgment are combined only through such a living act, whereas Frege postulates an already given judgeable content as the subject of the affirmation. This is closer in certain respect to Hermann Lotze who, in his *Logic* of 1874, distinguishes two thoughts in every judgment, the thought that constitutes the combination of ideas, the judgeable content, and in addition an 'auxiliary', second thought which affirms the so constituted content. Frege's own formulations in the *Begriffsschrift* make it clear that he disagrees with Lotze's postulation of two separate thoughts, one constituting the judgeable content and the other the judgment itself. In this respect he agrees with a third author, Julius Bergmann, who in his *Pure Logic* of 1879 attacked Lotze's doctrine of auxiliary thoughts and argued instead that judging is taking 'a critical stand to an idea.' And here the idea is taken as given and as a full judgeable content in Frege's sense. The same doctrine is expressed shortly after the *Begriffsschrift* in 1882 by Wilhelm Windelband, who speaks of a distinction between judgments (his name for Frege's judgeable contents) and acts of judging (*Beurteilungen*). Windelband writes:

> Every judgment expresses the thought that a specific idea (the subject of the judgment) is thought to stand in one of several possible relations . . . to a specific other idea (the predicate of the judgment). In an act of judging, however, we are adding the predicate expressing this act to an object which is represented or recognized as complete (the subject of expression of the act of judging). Through this . . . our feeling of approval or disapproval is expressed.[14]

If it strikes us as peculiar that the operation of judging is here described as the attachment of a predicate to a complete judgeable content, we must remind ourselves that this is, in fact, also the language Frege speaks in the *Begriffsschrift*. He writes there that we can consider the special sign expressing an act of judging, his

---

[14] Wilhelm Windelband, 'Was ist Philosophie?' (1882), reprinted in *Präludien* (Tübingen: J. C. B. Mohr, 1921), vol. 1, p. 30. The issue is discussed also in Windelband's 1884 essay 'Beiträge zur Theorie der negativen Urteile', in *Strassburger Abhandlungen zur Philosophie* (Freiburg and Tübingen, 1884).

judgment sign, as the single predicate in our language, a predicate which takes as its subject complete judgeable contents. According to Frege:

> Such a language would have only a single predicate for all judgments, namely, 'is a fact' . . . Our notation is a language of this sort, and in it the sign |– is the common predicate for all judgments. (p. 12–13)

Frege's early theory of judgments must thus be considered part of a contemporary discourse, largely conducted by philosophers associated with the renewal of Kantianism in the late nineteenth century.[15]

One of the peculiarities of the theory of judgment which Frege adopts from this philosophical context is that it calls for few semantic distinctions. There are words and sentences corresponding to the ideas and combinations of ideas that make up judgeable contents. But since Frege has no theory of truth, he is not in a position to ask whether judgeable contents should be thought to correspond to things in the world. Apart from distinguishing sign and content he allows himself only the observation that 'the same content can be completely determined in different ways.' This occurs, he thinks, when we have two names or two descriptions of the same content. He writes

---

[15] In *Gottlob Frege*, I had maintained that Frege's early theory of judgment was 'the Kantian theory in the particular form that Lotze had given it.' (p. 192, n. 45) I now realize that this was an oversimplification. The *Begriffsschrift* account of judgments diverges from Lotze's in that it makes no use of the idea of an auxiliary thought. The point has been made in Michael Dummett's essay 'Frege's 'Kernsätze zur Logik', *Frege and Other Philosophers* (Oxford: Clarendon Press, 1991).

While Dummett rightly stresses the importance of Frege's 'Kernsätze' for an understanding of his semantic views, he thoroughly overestimates the implications of his discovery. His interpretation seeks to show that while the piece reveals Frege's familiarity with Lotze's logic, it is also a devastating a critique of it and since, as Dummett argues, Frege composed the piece in 1876 or 1877, before he wrote the *Begriffsschrift*, Lotze had no positive significance for him once he began his constructive work. Dummett's conclusions strike me as rash. The piece shows at best that Frege rejected certain quite specific parts of Lotze's thought, not that he regarded him in general as 'a producer of extremely wordy and rather fuzzy philosophical writing' which is 'hardly ever sharply expressed or quite on target,' as Dummett puts it. (p. 78) What is more, Dummett's dating of the piece is unconvincing, Wolfgang Carl has recently argued with a great deal of plausibility that it must have been written 'before 1885', in other words, after the *Begriffsschrift*. (Carl, *loc. cit.*, p. 35 and n. 8) This conclusion seems confirmed by the fact that Frege casts his critique of Lotze's theory of judgment in terms of a notion of truth which is not yet employed in the *Begriffsschrift*. Once Frege's text is properly dated, we can see that, far from undermining the thesis that Lotze's logic was of positive importance to Frege, that it was of interest to him after he had set up his own logic and developed his own account of judgment.

that the existence of different names for the same content is not always merely an irrelevant matter of form; rather, that there are such names is the very heart of the matter if each is associated with a different way of determining the content.

And he adds to this the all important conclusion: 'In that case the judgment that has the identity of content as its object is synthetic, in the Kantian sense.' (p. 21)

It was this conclusion together with the theory of judgment that motivated it which Frege saw himself eventually forced to modify. These modifications resulted in his sense-reference semantics and in his reflections on the concept of truth. My claim is that the development was forced upon him by his evolving views about mathematics.

III

Some hints in Frege's doctoral dissertation and in his *Habilitationsschrift* indicate that he was already committed at the time to the double thesis that arithmetical laws are analytic and derivable from pure logic, while geometrical truths are synthetic a priori, i.e. necessarily true, though not on logical grounds. The logicist thesis is implied also in the preface of the *Begriffsschrift* where Frege confronts us with the question whether propositions of arithmetic can be justified 'by means of inferences alone, with the sole support of those laws of thought that transcend all particulars,' laws also characterized as 'laws upon which all knowledge rests' and indeed as laws of logic (p. 5). Five years before *The Foundations of Arithmetic* Frege seems already to be concerned with the double project of introducing more precise proof methods in mathematics and justifying an anti-empiricist epistemology. Accordingly, he concludes the preface to the *Begriffsschrift* with the announcement:

> Arithmetic was the point of departure for the train of thought that led me to my conceptual notation. And that is why I intend to apply it first of all to that science, attempting to provide a more detailed analysis of the concepts of arithmetic and a deeper foundation for its theorems. (p. 8)

But Frege did not, in fact, carry out this agenda. Instead, he published almost nothing for the following five years. And his next book, *The Foundations of Arithmetic*, did not continue on the track laid down in the *Begriffsschrift*, but engaged in a broad philosophical discussion of how the natural numbers might be defined. It was only fourteen years after the *Begriffsschrift*, in the first volume of the *Fundamental Laws of Arithmetic*, that Frege resumed his argument at the point at which his first book had left off. Given this history, we must ask what interrupted Frege's progress.

The answer is, in short, that he had come to see that the logic of the *Begriffsschrift* was insufficient for the reconstruction of arithmetic as a branch of logic. The problem, it turned out, was that of the definition of the natural numbers. We do not have any clear picture of how he had conceived of their definition in the *Begriffsschrift*. Our only hint is his statement: 'My initial step was to attempt to reduce the concept of ordering in a sequence to that of *logical* consequence, so as to proceed from there to the concept of number.' (p. 5) Chapter 3 of the *Begriffsschrift* shows, indeed, how the notion of ordering in a sequence and specifically the notion of a progression are formally definable. We must assume that he thought at the time of the numbers as indices on the operations generating such progressions. That would make his account similar to Wittgenstein's in the *Tractatus* where we read that 'a number is the exponent of an operation,' (6.021)[16]

Frege did evidently not stay satisfied with this account. In *The Foundations of Arithmetic* he argued that numbers must be considered self-subsistent objects (something about which we can make identity claims) and since he still took arithmetic to be derivable from the laws of logic, he now saw himself compelled to postulate the existence of logical objects. The *Begriffsschrift* had, however, not provided for such things. Frege concluded that it needed to be supplemented by a theory of what he called extensions of concepts.

The apparent breakthrough affected by *The Foundations of Arithmetic* was followed by another silence, this time of no less than seven years. In the mean time Frege was evidently at work on his main treatise, *The Fundamental Laws of Arithmetic*, which was meant to establish the truth of the logicist thesis once and for all. But completion of that project demanded, as he came to realize, a number of further innovations. Above all, he needed to generalize and ground the notion of the extension of a concept, and he did so by introducing the notion of a value-range. A value-range of a function f is for Frege set-theoretically speaking a set of ordered pairs whose first element is a possible argument for f (or an ordered

---

[16] It is possible to read Wittgenstein's thoughts on these matters as a defence of Frege's earlier position against the one elaborated in *The Foundations of Arithmetic*.

set of n arguments, if f is an n-place function) and whose second element is the value of f for that argument (or for that ordered set of n arguments). A more recent set-theoretical terminology would call Frege's value-ranges 'graphs'.[17] The introduction of this new notion required, Frege concluded, the addition of a new axiom to the logic of the *Begriffsschrift*. He called it his axiom V in *The Fundamental Laws of Arithmetic*. Axiom V can be represented as follows:

$$(\grave{a}f(a) = \grave{e}g(e)) = (x)\ (f(x) = g(x))$$

It says that the value-range (or graph) of f is identical with the value-range (or graph) of g, if and only if the functions f and g have the same values for the same arguments. Classes or extensions of concepts are for Frege those value-ranges whose functions always generate a truth-value. In other words, an instance of axiom V is

$$\text{Va} \qquad (\grave{a}F(a) = \grave{e}G(e)) = (x)\ (F(x) = G(x))$$

where F and G are taken to designate truth-functions or, more colloquially speaking, concepts. Va says in essence that the extensions of two concepts are identical, if and only if their defining concepts are equivalent.

In *The Fundamental Laws of Arithmetic* Frege tried to show how the axiom system of the *Begriffsschrift* enriched by axiom V was sufficient to define all the basic concepts of arithmetic including the individual natural numbers and to derive all of Peano arithmetic. The only problem that might be foreseen, would be that of the validity of axiom V. But, he added, no one will be able to show that it is invalid.

Still, there remained a question which he did not explicitly raise in this context but which must have been uppermost in his mind. It is whether axiom V can be considered an analytic or logical truth. In Frege's eyes, axiom V constituted an identity statement, something he did not distinguish from a material equivalence. But the problem was that the *Begriffsschrift* account of identity statements clearly implied that axiom V was a synthetic truth and not an analytic one.

It was this crucial problem that forced on Frege the need for revision of the semantic conceptions of the *Begriffsschrift* and of the

---

[17] Frege himself would, of course, have rejected any set-theoretical characterization of the notion of value-range. The notions of function and value-range are for him more elementary than the notions of set theory and more clearly logical notions.

theory of judgment that supported it. Two things were obviously required: (1) The new account would have to focus on whole sentences, since the formulas on the two sides of the main identity sign in axiom V were sentence schemas and (2) it had to draw the distinction between logically true and empirically true identity statements of the form $p = q$ in a way that would make axiom V come out as a logical truth. Frege resolved the problem by postulating a distinction between the sense and the reference of a sentence and by declaring $p = q$ logically true, if p and q have the same sense, but empirically true, if they have only the same reference.

But did he, in fact, assume that the two sides of axiom V have the same sense? In his essay on 'Function and Concept' he wrote of a specific instance of axiom V that its right-hand side 'expresses the same sense' as the left-hand side, 'but in a different way.' And in further explanation he said: 'It presents the sense as an equality holding generally; whereas the newly-introduced expression is simply an equation.' On the *Begriffschrift* account, the two expressions would be said to represent the same content, but they would do so, as he still acknowledged at this later point, 'in a different way.' Axiom V would for that reason be indubitably synthetic. According to the new account, two expressions that represent something in different ways may still be said to express the same sense. Identity statements in which the two expressions have the same sense are now to be considered logically true. Frege's reasoning is not difficult to follow. We generally regard identity-statements as analytic and logically true, if the expressions on the two sides of the identity sign are synonymous. Frege's notion of sameness of sense is meant to make our intuitive notion of synonymy more precise. If the expressions on the two sides if the identity sign in axiom V have, indeed, the same sense, it must follow that the axiom expresses an analytic truth. Frege himself concluded, in fact, that axiom V 'must be taken to be a fundamental law of logic.'[18]

There remained for him the question how the new account of meaning was to be worked out. Here he relied on terms previously coined by Lotze and Windelband. From Lotze's *Logik* he borrowed the terminology of calling the senses of sentences 'thoughts' – a

---

[18] Gottlob Frege, 'Function and Concept', Peter Geach and Max Black, eds., *Translations from the Philosophical Writings of Gottlob Frege* (Oxford: Basil Blackwell, 3rd ed., 1980), pp. 26–27. Frege is arguing here about a particular instance of what he will subsequently call axiom V, but the argument will surely carry over to that axiom itself.

somewhat unusual use of language insofar as these thoughts were considered by both Frege and Lotze not to be mental contents, but their supposed objective correlates. For his account of the references of sentences Frege turned to the Neo-Kantian philosopher Wilhelm Windelband.[19] When Windelband had discussed the distinction between judgeable contents (or judgments, as he had called them) and acts of judging some ten years earlier, he had at the same time characterized judging as a transition from the judgement (i.e., the judgeable content) to something for which he had coined the term 'truth-value' (*Wahrheitswert*). 'All sentences making knowledge claims,' Windelband had written, 'are combinations of ideas whose truth-value is already decided through the affirmation or negation.'[20] In spelling out his sense-reference distinction, Frege found it convenient to adapt Windelband's account for his own purposes. He concluded that a sentence's being true or false had to count as the reference of a sentence, and, following Windelband, he called these references truth-values. Judgment, he said in 'On Sense and Reference', is 'the advance from the thought to its truth-value.'[21] And echoing Windelband's words he added that 'in every judgement . . . the step from the level of thoughts to the level of reference (the objective) has already been taken.' (p. 64)

The affinities between Frege's and Windelband's reasoning become even more evident when we turn to Heinrich Rickert, Windelband's student, and his 1892 book *The Object of Knowledge*. Published in the same year as Frege's essay 'On Sense and Reference', that work elaborated Windelband's doctrine of judgeable contents and truth-values. In order to make the distinction between a judgeable content and a judgment plausible, Rickert proposed a test that was subsequently adopted by Frege. It was to change every assertion of the form 'The sun is shining' into the form 'Is the sun shining? Yes' thereby separating content from judgment. Rickert went on to say that in every judgment a value is affirmed, i.e. truth or falsity, a value which attaches timelessly to the content of the judgment. Truth and falsity are values in the strictest sense of the word, and it is for this reason that we find it appropriate to take a positive or negative stand to judgeable

---

[19] Frege's connections with Windelband's and Rickert's ideas were first noted by Gottfried Gabriel 'Frege als Neukantianer', *Kantstudien*, vol. 77, 1986, pp. 84–101.

[20] 'Was ist Philosophie?', loc. cit., p. 32.

[21] Geach and Black, loc. cit., p. 78.

contents that have these values. The object of our knowledge, Rickert went on to argue, is not things in the world of facts, but truth itself conceived as a positive value. The truth-values were in fact both objects and values at the same time. Rickert also suggested that the truth-value True might be conceived as the totality of all judgments recognized to have a positive value. (p. 83) The suggestion recalls Frege's idea in the *Fundamental Laws of Arithmetic* that it might be possible to characterize the True as the class of all true propositions and the False as the class of all false ones. But this is surely not the only point of comparison between Frege's and Rickert's views. Among the similarities is also the idea that truth is not a derivative characteristic of judgments, but basic and indefinable. As Rickert puts it, true judgments are not true 'because what they say is real, but we call real what is recognized as true by our judgments.' (p. 64) Rickert holds moreover in agreement with Frege that truth attaches to our judgments whether or not we recognize it. And like Frege he argues that relativism and skepticism must fail, because the relativist must implicitly acknowledge absolute truth in asserting his relativism. I believe also that Frege, like Rickert, assumed truth and falsity to be values in the normative (not only in the mathematical) sense and that, once again like Rickert, he assumed that this would explain why we aim at truth rather than falsity in our thinking.

IV

My point is then that Frege's semantics of thoughts and truth-values, far from being original, is to a considerable extent a quotation, a borrowing from Lotze, Windelband, and possibly Rickert. And this is of interest when we try to locate Frege in a wider historical context. For these men were all connected with the neo-Kantian movement in philosophy and, in particular, with the so-called South-West Germany branch of neo-Kantianism.[22] Given these connections, it seems plausible to link Frege's name to this movement in German philosophy. A caveat is, however, in place. The fact that Frege borrowed certain concepts and ideas from Lotze, Windelband, and Rickert does not mean that he bought

---

[22] So-called because Windelband and Rickert taught at Strassburg and Heidelberg, not because these philosophers came originally from the South-West of Germany. Another figure connected with that group was the philosopher Bruno Bauch, Frege's colleague and associate in Jena.

wholesale into their philosophical systems. It is precisely in the nature of such borrowings that they are partial.[23]

As far as Frege is concerned, it remains true that his primary concern was with mathematics and that he largely ignored what did not fit his agenda. This can also explain why this treatment of questions of meaning is so selective and, from a contemporary point of view, so incomplete. It is worth recalling here that the essays 'On Concept and Object', 'Function and Concept', and 'On Sense and Reference,' in which he concerned himself in the most sustained way with questions of meaning, appeared shortly before the first volume of his main work, *The Fundamental Laws of Arithmetic*. Though self-contained in tone, they should, presumably, be read as preparatory studies for the latter work.

But to recognize that questions of meaning were of secondary concern for Frege does not mean that he did not seriously adhere to the views which he laid out or that they may not have had an intrinsic interest to him. The point is of particular significance when we turn to Frege's thinking after Russell had communicated the logical antinomy derivable from axiom V of the *Fundamental Laws of Arithmetic*. The discovery brought Frege's attempt to reduce arithmetic to logic to an unhappy end. He now returned to the logic of the *Begriffsschrift* which he considered secure; at the same time he took obvious comfort from the views on meaning which he had worked out in the early 1890's. Where he had thought about them previously as tools for his foundational investigations, they now took on an independent interest for him. Our picture of Frege as preoccupied with questions of meaning corresponds, thus, to one which he himself may have found attractive in this phase of his life. It was in these years also that Rudolf Carnap came to be Frege's student and that Wittgenstein visited him at Jena. This suggests the possibility that the picture of Frege as predominantly a philosopher of language and meaning, passed on to us by Wittgenstein and Carnap, was in part his own creation. But even at this late point Frege had, of course, not abandoned his original foundational and anti-empiricist agenda. We know from his posthumously published notes, that in the last two years of his life he set out anew to dislodge the empiricist view of knowledge, trying this time to ground arithmetic in geometry and both in what he

---

[23] I state this caveat here in order to distance myself from a characterization of Frege as a transcendental idealist which I once gave – though not in my book – and which critics have frequently, and, it seems to me, unfairly focused on.

considered a non-empirical source of knowledge – the a priori intuition of space and time. The original program that had motivated him was, so it seems, still intact.

V

One last thought needs to be made clear. Throughout my discussion I have resisted any talk of Frege's *theory* of meaning. For I do not believe that Frege intended to propose a formal theory of meaning. On the contrary, he considered any such theory impossible and this is, of course, the strongest reason for rejecting the claim that he was at heart a theorist of meaning.

We can reconstruct Frege's antitheoretical position most easily by introducing three auxiliary notions. I say that

(1) *x* and *y* are categorially distinct if and only if there is no predicate that can meaningfully be applied to both *x* and *y*.
(2) A predicate is *categorially illicit* if and only if it is assumed to apply to some *x* and some *y* that are categorially distinct.
(3) A predicate is *categorially defective* if and only if it is defined in terms of predicates that are categorially illicit.

Categorial distinctions are not unknown in philosophy. Medieval thinkers, for instance, argued frequently that the distinction between God and man is categorial in our sense. This claim lies behind such enterprises as negative and analogical theology. Russell's theory of types also relies on categorial distinctions; there is for that reason, as Wittgenstein recognized, strictly speaking no such thing as a *theory* of types.

Now it is obvious in Frege's case, that the distinction between functions and objects is for him a categorial one. For he argues that there is no predicate which can be meaningfully predicted of both functions and objects. It follows that we can given no theoretical account of the semantics of names and functional expressions. For in order to do that, we would have to say that names refer to objects but not to functions and that functional expressions refer to functions and not to objects. The predicates 'being an object', 'being a function', as well as the relation '*x* refers to *y*' are categorially illicit, as Frege acknowledges in a number of places. Since, moreover, any account of the meaning of sentences would have to be given in terms of an account of the meanings of their constituent names and functional expressions, it follows that there cannot be a formal theory of sentence meanings. Any definition of the concept of truth, any attempt to determine its content, presupposes predicates which are categorially illicit. The concept of truth must therefore be considered categorially defective.

To this one must add that the notions of categorial distinctness, categorial illicitness, and categorial defectiveness are themselves categorially illicit or defective. The attempt to say that x and y are categorially distinct would supply us with a predicate that could meaningfully be predicated of both x and y. But by assumption, there is no such predicate. It follows that the three notions can be considered only auxiliary devices for making certain intuitive insights more transparent; they are not concepts that could function in a formally correct proof. In other words, just as there can be no formal theory of meaning according to Frege, there can also be no formal proof of the impossibility of such a theory. That is, presumably, the ultimate reason why he never tried to construct such a proof.

How then are we to understand Frege's own remarks about the meanings of names, functional expressions, and sentences? In the way he himself has indicated: as practical hints that get us to grasp the functioning of our language and to make the transition from our imperfect everyday language to the more perfect language of the logical calculus. As he himself put it in reference to the notion of truth:

> How is it then that this word 'true', though it seems devoid of content, cannot be dispensed with? Would it not be possible, at least in laying the foundations of logic, to avoid this word altogether? That we cannot do so is due to the imperfection of language. If our language were logically more perfect we would perhaps have no further need of logic, or we might read it off from the language.[24]

Department of Philosophy
University of California, Berkeley
Berkeley, California 94720–2390
USA

---

[24] 'My basic logical insights', in Gottlob Frege, *Posthumous Writings* (Chicago: University of Chicago Press, 1979), p. 252. I am grateful to Ernie LePore, Leon Henkin, William Craig, Matthew Henken, Michael Idinopoulos, and David Cerbone and commentators at the University of Toronto and the University of California at Riverside for critical remarks on versions of this paper.

III

WAS RUSSELL AN ANALYTICAL PHILOSOPHER?

Ray Monk

In an influential paper entitled 'Can Analytical Philosophy be Systematic and Ought it to Be?', Michael Dummett has endeavoured to specify what, exactly, analytical philosophy *is*. His answer is that it is 'post-Fregean philosophy'. 'We may characterise analytical philosophy', he writes, 'as that which follows Frege in accepting that the philosophy of language is the foundation for the rest of the subject':

> For Frege, as for all subsequent analytical philosophers, the philosophy of language is the foundation of all other philosophy, because it is only by the analysis of language that we can analyse thought.[1]

By the end of the paper, this characterisation has become the basis for a piece of unashamed dogmatism. 'Only with Frege', Dummett now declares, 'was the proper object of philosophy finally established: namely, first, that the goal of philosophy is the analysis of the structure of *thought*; secondly, that the study of *thought* is to be sharply distinguished from the study of the psychological process of *thinking*; and, finally, that the only proper method of analysing thought consists in the analysis of *language*. . . . the acceptance of these three tenets is common to the entire analytical school'.[2]

In his more recent books, *Frege: Philosophy of Mathematics* and *Origins of Analytical Philosophy*, Dummett has shown how seriously and literally he takes this dogma. 'Analytical philosophy was born when the "linguistic turn" was taken'[3] he insists, and the linguistic turn was taken, he further claims, by Frege, in 1884. Indeed, in his view, it is possible to be even more specific. The linguistic turn, the decisive step towards an understanding of 'the proper object of philosophy' was taken in paragraph §62 of *Die Grundlagen der Arithmetik*, where Frege, having begun by asking about the nature of number, ends by asking instead about the meanings of sentences containing number words. '*There* is the linguistic turn', Dummett

[1] Michael Dummett, *Truth and other Enigmas* (London: Duckworth, 1978), pp. 441–2.
[2] Ibid, p. 458.
[3] Michael Dummett, *Origins of Analytical Philosophy* (London: Duckworth, 1993), p. 5.

exclaims, 'The context principle is stated as an explicitly linguistic one, a principle concerning the meanings of words and their occurrence in sentences; and so an epistemological problem, with ontological overtones, is by its means converted into one about the meanings of sentences.[4] It is, Dummett claims, 'arguably the most pregnant philosophical paragraph ever written . . . If it were on the strength of *Grundlagen* §62, and its sequel alone, he [Frege] would still deserve to be rated the grandfather of analytical philosophy.'[5]

This pregnant paragraph gave birth to what Dummett later calls the 'fundamental axiom of analytical philosophy – that the only route to the analysis of thought goes through the analysis of language'[6]. In Dummett's view, philosophers who reject this axiom are not, properly speaking, analytical philosophers at all, even if they have been trained and brought up within the analytical tradition. Gareth Evans, for example, was, in Dummett's estimation, 'no longer an analytical philosopher', after he had tried, in *Varieties of Reference*, in Dummett's words, to give 'an account, independent of language, of what it is to think about an object in each of various ways'.[7]

In this paper I want to make clear that Evans is here in good company, that Bertrand Russell, generally considered – even by Dummett – one of the founders of the analytical tradition, would also fail, on Dummett's description, to count as an analytical philosopher. This, I regard as a *reductio ad absurdum* of Dummett's characterisation of the analytical tradition, which, I suggest, might be improved by relaxing its preoccupation with the 'linguistic turn', and giving more weight to what, in his various attempts to characterise analytical philosophy, Dummett rather curiously ignores: analysis.

In his old age, Russell demonstrated in several reviews and articles his extreme hostility to the type of philosophy that prevailed in England in the nineteen-fifties under the influence of the later Wittgenstein. 'In common with all philosophers before [the later Wittgenstein]', he wrote, 'my fundamental aim has been to understand the world as well as may be, and to separate what may count as knowledge from what must be rejected as unfounded opinion': 'But we are now told that it is not the world that we are to

[4] Michael Dummett, *Frege: Philosophy of Mathematics* (London: Duckworth, 1991), p. 111.
[5] Ibid., p. 112.
[6] *Origins*, op. cit., p. 128.
[7] Ibid., p. 4.

try to understand but only sentences'.[8] In its excessive preoccupation with language, Russell felt, this type of philosophy had 'abandoned, without necessity, that grave and important task which philosophy throughout the ages has hitherto pursued. Philosophers from Thales onwards have tried to understand the world . . . I cannot feel that the new philosophy is carrying on this tradition'.[9]

This attitude is surely as far removed as it is possible to be from Dummett's view that, in its concentration on language, analytical philosophy has discovered for the first time the 'proper subject for philosophy.' And it is not, as is sometimes thought, merely the querulous outpourings of an embittered old man who finds himself out of favour with the younger generation. Russell *never* thought that the study of language was the foundation of all other philosophy.

In *An Inquiry into Meaning and Truth*, the only book Russell devoted to questions of meaning and language, he insists again and again that his fundamental aim in the book is epistemological. The book begins with the declaration that: 'The present work is intended as an investigation of certain problems concerning empirical knowledge'[10]. And on the following page, he says: 'Our problem is one in the theory of knowledge'[11]. Several times throughout the book, he attacks logical positivists for their 'linguistic bias', which, he feels, prevents them from giving due emphasis to the non-linguistic features of experience. It is true that Russell, for epistemological reasons, offers a general theory of meaning in this book, but it is not such as would recommend itself to Dummett. Indeed, in reversing what Dummett takes to be the 'relative priority of thought and language', it is one that would immediately consign Russell to the deviant school of non-analytical philosophers to which Dummett would despatch Gareth Evans and Christopher Peacocke. Russell, in fact, goes much further than Evans or Peacocke. For he even defines what a proposition is in psychological terms:

. . . it is necessary to distinguish propositions from sentences, but . . . propositions need not be indefinable. They are to be defined

[8] Bertrand Russell, *My Philosophical Development* (New York: Simon and Schuster, 1959), p. 217.
[9] Ibid., p. 230.
[10] Russell, *An Inquiry into Meaning and Truth* (London: Unwin Paperbacks, 1980), p. 11.
[11] Ibid., p. 12.

as psychological occurrences of certain sorts – complex images, expectations, etc. Such occurrences are 'expressed' by sentences . . . When two sentences have the same meaning, that is because they express the same proposition. Words are not essential to propositions. The exact psychological definition of propositions is irrelevant to logic and theory of knowledge; the only thing essential to our inquiries is that sentences signify something other than themselves, which can be the same when the sentences differ. That this something is psychological (or physiological) is made evident by the fact that propositions can be false.[12]

In *My Philosophical Development*, Russell writes that it was not until 1918 that he first became interested in 'the definition of "meaning" and in the relation of language to fact'. 'Until then', he says, 'I had regarded language as "transparent" '[13]. And, from that time on, he believed that, as he puts it in his 'Lectures of Logical Atomism': 'the notion of meaning is always more or less psychological, and that it is not possible to get a pure logical theory of meaning, nor therefore of symbolism'[14]. The theory of symbolism, he says in those lectures, is important to philosophy – 'a good deal more than one time I thought' – but its importance is 'entirely negative':

i.e., the importance lies in the fact that unless you are fairly self-conscious about symbols, unless you are fairly aware of the relation of the symbol to what it symbolizes, you will find yourself attributing to the thing properties which only belong to the symbol.[15]

The 'de-psychologising' of logic that Michael Dummett takes to be central to analytical philosophy – and which he takes to go hand in hand with the adoption of the philosophy of language as the central concern of philosophers – was something that Russell took part in *until* he became interested in the theory of meaning. 'The problem of meaning', he wrote in 1938 (in an Aristotelian Society debate with Richard Braithwaite on 'The Relevance of Psychology to Logic'), was what 'first led me . . . to abandon the anti-psychological opinions in which I had previously believed'[16].

[12] Ibid., p. 189.
[13] *My Philosophical Development*, op. cit., p. 145.
[14] Russell, *Lectures on Logical Atomism* (La Salle: Open Court, 1985), p. 45.
[15] Ibid., p. 44.
[16] *Aristotelian Society, Supplementary Volume*, 17 (1938), p. 43.

'I hold that in a critical scrutiny of what passes for knowledge', he said later in the same paper, 'the ultimate point is one where doubt is psychologically impossible, whereas he [Braithwaite] holds that it is one where doubt is logically absurd'[17].

Curiously enough, this 'psychologistic turn' in Russell's thinking went hand in hand with his conviction by Wittgenstein that logic was essentially linguistic. Right up until 1919, until that is, immediately before his reading of Wittgenstein's *Tractatus*, Russell had held on to a conception of logic that saw it as the investigation of the most general features, not of language, but of the world. Logic, he says, in *Introduction to Mathematical Philosophy*, 'is concerned with the real world just as truly as zoology, though with its more abstract and general features'.[18] Logic is the study of the formal characteristics *of the world*. An interest in language is necessary, only to realise the inadequacy of ordinary language to express logical form with any kind of exactitude and the consequent necessity to master the specialised language of mathematical logic.

This view of logic is also contained in the 'Lectures on Logical Atomism' given at about the same time. Logic, Russell says there, is 'concerned with the forms of facts, with getting hold of the different sorts of facts . . . that there are in the world'.[19] These forms are extremely rarefied aspects of reality, so rarefied that it is almost impossibly difficult to think about them at all. In philosophical logic, he says, 'the subject matter that you are supposed to be thinking of is so exceedingly difficult and elusive that any person who has ever tried to think about it knows that you do not think about it except perhaps once in six months for half a minute. The rest of the time you think about the symbols'.[20] The really good philosopher is the one who succeeds in focusing his mind on this exceedingly refined subject matter once in six months: 'Bad philosophers never do'.[21]

The contrast that is here so crucial to Russell between thinking about symbols and thinking about logical forms is, of course, precisely the one that Dummett regards analytical philosophy – and all sound philosophy – to have given up. Russell himself gave it up about a year later, when he read the *Tractatus* and discussed it with

[17] Ibid., p. 51.
[18] Russell, *An Introduction to Mathematical Philosophy* 2nd ed. (London: George Allen & Unwin, 1920), p. 169.
[19] *Lectures on Logical Atomism*, op. cit., p. 80.
[20] Ibid., p. 44.
[21] Ibid.

Wittgenstein at their meeting in Holland at the end of 1919. The importance Wittgenstein's book had for Russell was to persuade him for the first time that logic and mathematics were linguistic and *therefore* entirely trivial. Just days after his meeting with Wittgenstein, Russell wrote a review of Harold Joachim's Inaugural Lecture, in which he declared roundly: 'As for logic and the so-called "Laws of Thought", they are concerned with symbols, they give different ways of saying the same thing . . . only an understanding of language is necessary in order to know a proposition of logic'.[22] Though it sounds in the context of the review as though this is an opinion that he had held all his life – an obvious truth of which only idiots and Professors of Logic at Oxford could possibly be ignorant – it is in fact one of which he had been persuaded for only a few days and one that contradicts views that he had published not twelve months previously.

It was, moreover, a deeply disillusioning belief. Far from establishing philosophy on its proper basis, the belief that logic and mathematics were linguistic, stripped them of all the interest that Russell had previously thought they possessed, and he rarely again thought or wrote about logic, mathematics or the philosophy of them. 'I have come to believe', he wrote in *My Philosophical Development*, 'though very reluctantly, that it [mathematics] consists of tautologies. I fear that, to a mind of sufficient intellectual power, the whole of mathematics would appear trivial, as trivial as the statement that a four-footed animal is an animal'.[23] For fifteen years after his meeting with Wittgenstein, he more or less gave up philosophy altogether, and, when he returned to it in the mid nineteen-thirties, it was to discuss, not logic and mathematics, but psychology, physics and epistemology.

Russell, then, after 1920 would have denied all three of the 'tenets' that Dummett regards as 'common to the entire analytical school': the goal of philosophy, he would have held, is not the analysis of thought, but the attempt to understand the world; the study of *thought*, of meanings, he would have said was, at bottom, psychological; and, far from accepting that the only proper method of analysing thought was the analysis of language, he would have maintained, on the contrary, that the only proper way of analysing language was to investigate thought, that the theory of meaning is a branch of psychology.

[22] Russell, 'The Wisdom of Our Ancestors', *The Collected Papers of Bertrand Russell 9* (London: Unwin Hyman, 1988), pp. 403–6.
[23] *My Philosophical Development*, op. cit., pp. 211–12.

And yet, despite all this, Russell would have called himself an analytical philosopher. His *History of Western Philosophy* ends, after all, with a proselytising chapter on 'the philosophy of logical analysis', which, however, he understands very differently than does Michael Dummett. On Russell's characterisation, 'the philosophy of logical analysis' is not primarily concerned with the theory of meaning, it is concerned rather with such questions as: what is number? what are space and time? what is mind? and what is matter? And its origins do not lie in the 'linguistic turn' of Frege's *Grundlagen*, but rather in the work of Weierstrass, Dedekind and Cantor in transforming 'Calculus' into 'Analysis'. 'The origin of this philosophy', he writes, 'is in the achievements of mathematicians who set to work to purge their subject of fallacies and slipshod reasoning':

> Weierstrass, soon after the middle of the nineteenth century, showed how to establish the calculus without infinitesimals, and thus at last made it logically secure. Next came Georg Cantor, who developed the theory of continuity and infinite number. 'Continuity' has been, until he defined it, a vague word, convenient for philosophers like Hegel, who wished to introduce metaphysical muddles into mathematics. Cantor gave a precise significance to the word, and showed that continuity, as he defined it, was the concept needed by mathematicians and physicists. By this means a great deal of mysticism . . . was rendered antiquated.[24]

It is frequently believed that the primary influence on Russell in the creation of the analytical tradition was G. E. Moore, but, in the last chapter of the *History*, in outlining analytical philosophy, though he pays tribute to Frege, Russell never once mentions either Moore or Wittgenstein. Though there may have been some personal reasons for this, it also, I believe, reflects faithfully what Russell considered important in the creation of analytical philosophy, at least as regards his own philosophical development.

Russell once said that there had only been one major revolution in his philosophical development, one great division in his work, and that was when he abandoned Hegelianism. One way of describing this revolution would be to say that it was when he abandoned the method of synthesis in favour of that of analysis,

[24] Russell, *History of Western Philosophy*, 2nd ed. (London: George Allen & Unwin, 1961), p. 783.

when he at last became persuaded that analysis was *not*, after all, falsification. There are, Russell was fond of saying, just two types of philosophers: those that think of the world as a bowl of jelly and those who think of it as a bucket of shot. The great revolution in his thinking came when he himself gave up the jelly in favour of the shot.

Hegel, of course, was the jelly philosopher *par excellence*, and Russell's mention of the metaphysical muddles introduced into mathematics by Hegel in the above description of the origin of analytical philosophy is no random example. His earliest thinking about mathematics was guided precisely by those muddles. 'Hegel thought of the universe as a closely knit unity', Russell writes in his essay 'Why I took to Philosophy':

> His universe was like a jelly in the fact that, if you touched any one part of it, the whole quivered; but it was unlike a jelly in the fact that it could not really be cut up into parts. The appearance of consisting of parts, according to him, was a delusion. The only reality was the Absolute, which was his name for God. In this philosophy I found comfort for a time. As presented to me by its adherents, especially McTaggart, who was then an intimate friend of mine, Hegel's philosophy had seemed both charming and demonstrable.[25]

In his *Studies of Hegelian Dialectic*, published in 1896, at the height of his influence upon Russell and of Russell's own Hegelianism, McTaggart emphasises the synthetic, interconnectedness of the world of Hegel's dialectic. Separateness is an illusion. The dialectic proceeds from the lower categories of understanding – things like space, time and matter – to the highest, the Absolute. Only this is indepedent and real, and only this is rational; all the lower categories are enmeshed in contradictions which are resolved by successive synthesis until one reaches the Absolute. Thus, logic shows us that 'all reality is rational and righteous . . . the highest object of philosophy is to indicate to us the general nature of a ultimate harmony, the full content of which it has not yet entered into our hearts to conceive. All true philosophy must be mystical, not indeed in its methods, but in its final conclusions'.[26]

This is the conception of philosophy that motivated Russell's

---

[25] Russell, *Portraits from Memory* (London: George Allen & Unwin, 1956), p. 21.
[26] J. M. E. McTaggart, *Studies in the Hegelian Dialectic* (Cambridge: Cambridge University Press, 1896), pp. 255, 259.

earliest work. Emotionally, he shook himself free of its influence at the end of 1897, when, in a paper written for the Apostles called 'Seems, Madam? Nay, it is', he robustly rejected the religious comforts of such a doctrine, together with the idea that it is the task of philosophy to provide such comforts. 'Why not admit', the paper concludes, 'that metaphysics, like science, is justified by intellectual curiosity, and ought to be guided by intellectual curiosity alone?'[27]

And yet, intellectually, he remained for a while longer in the grip – or perhaps in the sticky embrace – of the jelly-like world. On 1 January 1898, just two weeks after his Apostles paper, Russell wrote some notes 'On the Idea of a Dialectic of the Sciences' reaffirming his ambition of 'turning Appearance into Reality', of arriving at a view of the world *sub specie aeternitatis* through a succession of antinomies. Central to this ambition were the contraditions in mathematics he had been wrestling with for the previous few years: those of the infinitesimal, of continuity, and of the infinite.

The contradictions of the infinitesimal were those that had been pointed out with tenacity, vividness and a certain relish by Berkeley in *The Analyst*: the contradictions of first supposing the differential in the calculus to be an infinitely small quantity and then proceeding as if it were nothing at all, of regarding the infinitesimal as neither a something nor as a nothing but, in his glorious phrase, as 'the ghosts of departed quantities'. This contradiction was well-known, and Russell spent little time on it other than assuming that no answer to it had been provided by mathematicians. The contradictions of continuity were even older, having been exploited by Zeno in his Parmenidean arguments against motion. They turn on the impossibility of regarding a continuous quantity as a succession of points without thereby destroying its continuity. In an article written in 1896 called 'On Some Difficulties of Continuous Quantity', Russell raised these ancient objections to continuity and declared that 'philosophical antinomies, in this sphere, find their counterpart in mathematical fallacies. These fallacies seem, to me at least, to pervade the Calculus, and even the more elaborate machinery of Cantor's collections'.[28]

Russell, of course, came later to accept Cantor's solution to the

---

[27] *The Collected Papers of Bertrand Russell 1* (London: George Allen & Unwin, 1983), p. 111.
[28] *Collected Papers of Bertrand Russell 2* (London: Unwin Hyman, 1990), p. 46.

problem of continuity as one of the greatest intellectual achievements of our age, but, in 1896, still wedded to Hegelianism, he dismissed Cantor's transfinite numbers as 'impossible and self-contradictory'. Indeed, at this stage, he thought the concept of infinity itself to be riddled with contradictions, including the paradox pointed out by Leibniz that an infinite series can be put into a one-to-one correspondence with a proper subset of itself. For example, to every natural number can be assigned an even number, so, to the extent, both sets are infinite and have the same cardinality. But we know that there are more natural numbers than even numbers, and therefore that they *can't* have the same cardinality.

To a Hegelian, to whom mathematics is but one rung on the ladder to metaphysics, these contradictions are meat and drink, and Russell, for the moment, did not infer from them that the foundations of mathematics stood in need of improvement, but rather that mathematics itself was inherently flawed as a means of understanding reality.

The high point of Russell's Hegelianism, and a paper that shows just how jelly-like he was prepared to allow his world to become – and how far he was prepared to go in rejecting the truth of any kind of analysis of the world – is a short discussion document he wrote in the summer of 1897 called 'Why do we regard time, but not space as necessarily a plenum?'. The short answer, he told his wife Alys, is: 'Because we're fools'.[29] The long answer outlined in the paper – which was, it seems, written for discussion with Moore – is that we are mislead into thinking that space is analysable into relations between material objects, but we understand intuitively that time is plenal, that there are no gaps in time and therefore that time cannot be understood as a sequence of relations. But, Russell urges, what is true of time is true of space. Space, too, is a plenum: every bit of it is used up by matter in one form or another. Thus, argues Russell, the difference between relations and adjectives breaks down:

> On a strictly monistic view, ... no such distinction can be maintained. Everything is really an adjective of the One, an intrinsic property of the Universe; the Universe is not validly analyzable into simple elements at all.[30]

[29] Russell to his wife, Alys, 1.6.1897.
[30] *Collected Papers of Bertrand Russell 2*, op, cit., p. 95.

One thing that is revealed by this essay, and by almost everything Russell wrote at this time, is what he thought analysis was. Analysis, on his understanding, consisted in the identification of the parts of a whole. If reality was indivisible, it followed immediately that analysis was an invalid procedure.

One can see from reading such early essays the truth of Russell's later insistence that, unlike Moore, it was not Idealism from which he needed to be liberated so much as monism. In standard histories of philosophy, the role of Moore in Russell's intellectual development, and, in particular, of his creation of (his version of) analytical philosophy, is often wildly exaggerated. Moore *was* important, as I hope to show later, in providing Russell with an alternative conception of logic that matched his new-found faith in analysis, but it did nothing to *create* that faith. What created it, rather, was Russell's growing understanding and appreciation of the work in the foundations of mathematics that had been done in the middle of the nineteenth century.

Had Russell studied mathematics as an undergraduate at Berlin, or Jena or Göttingen, he would have been trained in a tradition of mathematical analysis that specifically addressed itself to the contradictions in the Calculus that he regarded as proof of Hegelianism, and had gone some way towards providing technical solutions to them. The epsilon-delta definition of continuity, for example, which used limits to provide a purely arithmetical understanding of continuity in a way that made no appeal to geometrical intuition and was free from formal contradiction, had been taught at German universities for twenty or thirty years. Cambridge however, was somewhat behind the times in its mathematics teaching, and Russell, to his later disgust, completed his mathematics degree in 1893 without knowing anything about these technical developments. He first heard of Weierstrass at the end of 1896 when he visited the United States and gave a series of lectures on non-Euclidean geometry. Two of the mathematicians who attended, Frank Morely and James Harkness, had previously been at Cambridge, but had acquired for themselves an education in modern pure mathematics which they later embodied in their textbook, *Introduction to the Theory of Analytic Functions*, which was published in 1898. Russell read their book soon after it was published and it had a great influence on him, but, more immediately, in his conversations with Morley, Harkness and others in America, he realized that there was a great deal of mathematics of philosophical interest of which he had remained ignorant.

After his visit to the States, and alongside his various attempts to understand mathematics along Hegelian lines, Russell read widely in the new mathematics, starting with Dedekind's *Continuity and Irrational Numbers* in December 1896. In the summer of 1897, the sense that there was more to be learnt from mathematicians than from philosophers about the nature of mathematics was confirmed by reading Hegel's *Logic* and being disgusted by its muddle-headedness. In the spring of 1898, this conviction was strengthened by his reading of Whitehead's *Universal Algebra*, from which, for the first time, he received a definition of mathematics that made no mention of 'quantity' and in which he saw, again for the first time, a *mathematical* treatment of symbolic logic. The following month, he read Dedekind's *The Nature and Meaning of Numbers*, from which, among other things, he learned to regard *order* rather than quantity as the central notion in the definition of number, and, thereby the irrelevance to mathematics of the antinomies of quantity upon which he spent so much time the previous year.

By the summer of the following year, having, by now, become soaked in the techniques of the new mathematics, the revolution in Russell's philosophical thinking was complete, and he began a book called *The Fundamental Ideas and Axioms of Mathematics*, much of which was later incorporated into *The Principles of Mathematics*. One of the things that distinguish this draft of a book from Russell's earlier work is its insistence on the reality of relations (and hence of plurality) and the legitimacy of analysis, though here he evidently still had residual doubts. 'Analysis', he writes, 'is strictly speaking, *only* possible in the case of such a combination as "A and B". Wherever there is a relation, wherever, that is, we have truth or falsehood, analysis is more or less destructive':

> A proposition may *contain* two terms and a relation, but is not simply equivalent to these. For the relation as such is a term, which does not relate anything. That something is lost by analysis appears from the fact that the whole is true or false, while the parts are neither. Thus the whole has a relation to either truth or falsehood, which its parts do not possess. And the same thing is evident from a mere consideration of meaning. 'A differs from B' is not equivalent to 'A and diversity and B'. Thus, wherever we have relations which actually relate, i.e. which are not used as terms, there analysis is not wholly legitimate.[31]

---

[31] Ibid., p. 299.

Something like this view survives in the final text of *Principles*, in Chapter XVI on 'Whole and Part'. There is, Russell says there, 'a very important logical doctrine, which the theory of whole and part brings into prominence':

> I mean the doctrine that analysis is falsification. Whatever can be analysed is a whole, and we have already seen that analysis of whole is in some measure falsification. But it is important to realise the very narrow limits of this doctrine. We cannot conclude that the parts of a whole are not really its parts, nor that the parts are not presupposed in the whole in a sense in which the whole is not presupposed in the parts, nor yet that the logically prior is not usually simpler than the logically subsequent. In short, though analysis gives us the truth, and nothing but the truth, yet it can never give us the whole truth. This is the only sense in which the doctrine is to be accepted. In any wider sense, it becomes merely a cloak for laziness, by giving an excuse to those who dislike the labour of analysis.[32]

Russell's faith that analysis was not *always* a falsification had been inspired chiefly by the success of the mathematical analysts in coping with the problems of the infinitesimal, the infinite and continuity, but he still needed a conception of logic – in particular a conception of the nature of a proposition – to replace that he had inherited from Hegelianism. And this is what G. E. Moore – in conversations with Russell in the summer of 1898 – and in his article 'The Nature of Judgment' – provided. In the Hegelian understanding, a proposition was a unity that defied analysis, on Moore's conception, it is a complex that positively cries out to be broken up into its constituent parts. 'A proposition', Moore writes, 'is nothing other than a complex concept ... A proposition is a synthesis of concepts ... A proposition is constituted by any number of concepts, together with a specific relation between them'.[33]

This looks like analytical philosophy in Dummett's sense of analysis of language, but, actually, for Moore, and especially for Russell, it was centrally important that propositions were *not* linguistic. 'A proposition', Moore says, 'is composed not of words, nor yet of thoughts, but of concepts. Concepts are possible objects of thought'.[34] Concepts, on Moore's view, are the building blocks,

[32] Russell, *The Principles of Mathematics*, op. cit., p. 141.
[33] G. E. Moore, *Selected Writings*, ed. Thomas Baldwin (London: Routledge, 1993), p. 5.
[34] Ibid., p. 4.

not of thought, but of the world. 'It seems necessary', he writes, 'to regard the world as formed of concepts'.[35] Thus, analysis is a method, not of understanding thought through language, but, so to speak, of carving up the world so that it begins to make some sort of sense: 'A thing becomes intelligible first when it is analysed into its constituent concepts',[36] writes Moore.

Russell's non-linguistic notion of a proposition astonished and bewildered Frege. In the course of their correspondence on the vexed subject of Russell's Paradox in 1902, Frege was moved to mention the fact that Russell seemed to use the word 'proposition' rather oddly. What is a proposition? he asked Russell. 'German logicians', he told Russell, 'understand by it the expression of a thought, a group of audible or visible signs expressing a thought. But you evidently mean the thought itself'.[37] He then outlined his theory of sense and reference as it applies to propositions. In reply, Russell was at first disinclined to be drawn into an involved discussion on the matter. 'I understand by a *proposition* its sense, not its truth-value', he told Frege, 'I cannot bring myself to believe that the true or the false is the meaning of a proposition in the same sense as, e.g., a certain person is the meaning of the name Julius Caesar'.[38] Later on, however, pressed by Frege, he was forced to elaborate:

> I still do not share your opinion about sense and meaning. I should like to say the following about them: In all cases, both imagination and judgement have an object: what I call a 'proposition' can be the object of judgment, and it can be the object of imagination. There are therefore two ways in which we can think of an object, in case this object is a complex: we can imagine it, or we can judge it; yet the object is the same in both cases.[39]

From here, it became clear to both of them how radically different were their understandings, not just of propositions, but also of thoughts. 'It seems to me', wrote Frege, 'that what you have in view is the difference between grasping a thought and recognizing it as true . . . Truth is not a component part of a thought, just as

[35] Ibid., p. 8.
[36] Ibid.
[37] Gottlob Frege, *Philosophical and Mathematical Correspondence* (Oxford: Blackwell, 1980), p. 149.
[38] Ibid., pp. 150–1.
[39] Ibid., p. 159.

Mont Blanc with its snowfields is not itself a component part of the thought that Mont Blanc is more than 4000 metres high'.[40]

'I believe', wrote Russell in reply, 'that in spite of all its snowfields Mont Blanc itself is a component part of what is actually asserted in the proposition "Mont Blanc is more than 4000 metres high". We do not assert the thought, for this is a private psychological matter: we assert the object of the thought, and this is, to my mind, a certain complex (an objective proposition, one might say) in which Mont Blanc is itself a component part. If we do not admit this, then we get the conclusion that we know nothing at all about Mont Blanc. This is why for me the *meaning* of a proposition is not the true, but a certain complex which (in the given case) is true . . . From what I have said about Mont Blanc you will see that I cannot accommodate the identity of all true propositions. For Mont Blanc is to my mind a component part of the proposition discussed above, but not of the proposition that all men are mortal. This alone proves that the two propositions are distinct from each other'.[41]

For Russell, then, a proposition was not anything linguistic; it was not a sentence, but the *meaning* of a sentence, which meant, for him, that it was a complex of objects. Thus, the analysis of propositions was not a linguistic exercise, but an ontological one; a question of identifying the objects in the complex. This, notoriously, made it insuperably difficult for him to understand what kind of complex a false proposition was. On his view, it would have to be a combination of objects that were not, in reality, so combined. But if they were not so combined, then there was no such thing. And so, Russell duly concluded that there was no such thing as a false proposition, from which it followed, he reasoned, that there were no true propositions either. Notice, that this entire chain of reasoning makes no sense whatever if a proposition is regarded as a sequence of words, or even of thoughts. For Russell, a proposition is, if anything, a sequence of objects. It cannot be so understood, so, therefore, there *are* no propositions.

By the time he finished *Principia Mathematica*, Russell had ended up with the view that the bearers of truth and falsehood were not propositions but *judgments*, and that these were to be analysed as multiple relations of objects and minds. This theory was famously demolished by Wittgenstein, sending Russell, in *The Analysis of*

[40] Ibid., p. 163.
[41] Ibid., p. 169.

Mind, in the direction of psychologism, thinking that a behaviouristic understanding of mental phenomena, in particular belief and judgement, would repair the hole Wittgenstein had knocked out of his philosophical logic. Russell's faith in this behaviouristic approach to the question of meaning was, as I said earlier, never shaken, even after he became convinced that logic and mathematics themselves were merely grammatical, syntactical (that, as he puts it in the *History*, that mathematical knowledge is 'all of the same nature as the "great truth" that there are three feet in a yard'[42]).

Throughout this entire, perhaps rather sorry development, throughout all its twists and turns, one thing remains absolutely constant. And that is the view that to analyse something is to identify its constituent parts, together with the conviction that progress in philosophy is not to be made by building systems, by the grand syntheses of the past, but by careful and minute examination of the grounds of our beliefs. Russell's greatest hope – and perhaps this is the one respect in which his conception of philosophy chimes with Dummett's – was that philosophy might, by adopting this analytical approach, aspire to a more systematic, co-operative 'scientific' method. Where he differs from Dummett, and from Dummett's Frege, is in whether this method should consist in the construction of a theory of meaning. But to deny, on the basis of this difference – as Dummett does implicitly if not explicitly – that Russell was an analytical philosopher seems perverse. He was, if nothing else, a believer in analysis. And that, probably, was the undoing of him.

Department of Philosophy
University of Southampton
Southampton SO17 1BJ
England

---

[42] *History of Western Philosophy*, op. cit., p. 786.

IV

THE RISE OF TWENTIETH CENTURY ANALYTIC PHILOSOPHY

P. M. S. Hacker

1. Analytic philosophy

If philosophy of the seventeenth and eighteenth centuries can be characterized as the age of reason and enlightenment, and philosophy of the nineteenth century as the age of historicism and historical self consciousness, then to that extent the twentieth century can be said to have been the age of language and logic. The role of exploring the philosophical consequences of the thought that man is above all a language using creature fell to analytic philosophy.[1] So too did the task of clarifying the significance of the unprecedentedly powerful formal logic invented at the turn of the century by Frege, Russell and Whitehead, and of elucidating the relations between logical calculi, language and thought.

Analytic philosophy came to dominate Anglophone, and for a while Viennese, and thence Scandinavian, philosophy from the 1920s until the 1970s. Modern analytic philosophy was born on the banks of the Cam at the turn of the century, whence its influence spread to the Danube and the Isis, and thence to far-flung countries across the globe. Many figures played a role in its development, but none a greater one than Ludwig Wittgenstein, who was one of the two major figures in the transformation of its first Moorean and Russellian phase into its second phase of Cambridge analysis in the 1920s. His influence moulded the third phase of Viennese logical positivism, and he was the leading inspiration of its fourth and final phase of connective[2] and therapeutic analysis which characterized post-war Oxford analytic philosophy.

This judgement is controversial. One ground of controversy is the very term 'analytic philosophy'. In a loose sense, one might say, all, or the bulk, of philosophy is analytic. Considered independently

---

[1] There were, of course, precursors, from Vico, through Hamann, Herder, Humboldt, and Schleiermacher to Dilthey.

[2] I owe the term 'connective analysis' to P. F. Strawson's *Analysis and Metaphysics, An Introduction to Philosophy* (Oxford: Oxford University Press, 1992), pp. 19–21.

of their antecedents and sources of inspiration, if Austin's investigations into excuses belong to analytic philosophy, then so too do Aristotle's investigations into voluntary action; if Ryle's writings upon the concept of mind are an example of analytic philosophy, so too are Aquinas's; if Strawson's writings on 'individuals' are a variety of analytic philosophy, then so too are Kant's on 'objects'. If the term 'analytic philosophy' is to be a useful classificatory term, it must do more work than merely to distinguish mainstream Western philosophy from the reflections of philosophical sages or prophets, such as Pascal or Nietzsche, and from the obscurities of speculative metaphysicians, such as Hegel, Bradley or Heidegger.

Professor Dummett has suggested that analytic philosophy is the philosophy of thought, and that its main tenet is that a philosophical account of thought can be obtained only through a philosophical account of language. This characterization is puzzling, since it is unclear what the 'philosophy of thought' might be. If 'thought' here means what Frege meant by 'Gedanke', then the philosophy of thought is simply the philosophy of, or a philosophical elucidation of, the concept of a proposition. But while the concept of a proposition is of great philosophical interest, and has been the subject of extensive philosophical controversy, it is hardly the whole of philosophy, or even of everything that might rightly be called 'analytic philosophy'. It is no more than a part of the philosophy of logic or philosophy of language. If 'thought' here means 'thinking', then the philosophy of thought is simply a part of philosophical psychology, and analytical philosophy of thought is no more than a fragment of analytical philosophy of psychology.

Dummett's explanation was tailored to fit Frege. 'Frege himself did not make the claim that the only task of analytic philosophy is the analysis of thought, and hence of language ...', Dummett admitted, 'but by his practice in the one particular branch of philosophy in which he worked, the philosophy of mathematics, he left little doubt that that was his view.[3] It seems to me that he left a great deal of doubt, that it is questionable whether Frege had *any general views* about the whole body of philosophy, whether he thought that analytic philosophy of psychology, of axiology, ethics and aesthetics, political and legal philosophy, etc. are all concerned with 'the analysis of thought, and hence of language'. Indeed,

---

[3] M. A. E. Dummett, 'Can Analytic Philosophy be Systematic and Ought It To Be?', repr. in his *Truth and Other Enigmas* (London: Duckworth, 1978), p. 442.

whether the cloth Dummett cut actually fits even the body of
Frege's own, very limited, philosophical concerns (i.e. the philosophy of mathematics and logic) is debatable, since Frege patently
did not think that an account of natural language was the best way
to investigate thoughts. On the contrary, he held that logic is the
science of the laws of thoughts, and that 'Someone who wants to
learn logic from language is like an adult who wants to learn how to
think from a child. When men created language, they were at a
stage of childish pictorial thinking. Languages are not made to
logic's ruler'.[4] Indeed, the task of the philosopher is to break the
power of the word over the human mind, to free thought 'from that
which only the nature of the linguistic means of expression attaches
to it'.[5] This exegetical question is controversial, but having
discussed it *in extenso* elsewhere,[6] I shall not debate this issue now.

Dummett's characterization of analytic philosophy is also meant
to capture the contours of the philosophy of Wittgenstein 'in all
phases of his career'.[7] This too seems to me to be wrong, and I shall
comment briefly on the matter. What is true is that according to the
early Wittgenstein of the *Tractatus*, the primary task of philosophy
was to determine the limits of thought by clarifying the essence of
the proposition as such. This was held to be the route to the
clarification of the essence of representation in general, and hence
of the essence of the world. But that idea marks a break with Frege
and Russell, not the continuation of an established tradition of
analytic philosophy. For according to Frege, a thought is an
abstract entity which exists in a 'third realm' of sempiternal
Platonic objects, whereas Wittgenstein conceived of a proposition
as a linguistic entity – a meaningful sentence. For Wittgenstein, but
not for Frege, the investigation into the nature of the proposition
was an investigation into the essential nature of representation by
means of symbols. Neither Frege nor Russell believed that the
philosophical investigation of logic was an investigation into the
essential nature of *symbolism*. True, Wittgenstein held that studying
the limits of language will also reveal the limits of thought – but the
limits of thought are the limits of the *thinkable*. He did not mean

---

[4] Frege, letter to Husserl, dated 30.10–1.11.1906, in his *Philosophical and Mathematical
Correspondence*, pp. 67f.

[5] G. Frege, *Conceptual Notation*, tr. and ed. T. W. Bynum (Oxford: Clarendon Press, 1972),
Preface.

[6] See G. P. Baker and P. M. S. Hacker, *Frege: Logical Excavations* (Oxford: Blackwell and
New York: University Press, 1984), chs. 1 and 3.

[7] M. A. E. Dummett, *Origins of Analytical Philosophy* (London: Duckworth, 1993), p. 4.

here by 'thought' what Frege meant (i.e. a proposition conceived as an abstract entity). Rather, he meant by 'thought' or 'proposition' the *sentence* in its projective relation to reality. On his view, an investigation of the essence of *any possible language* will disclose the limits of *what can be said*, and *hence* the limits of what can be thought.

That was a dramatic break with his predecessors. But given that transformation, it would have been trivial for Wittgenstein to suggest that a philosophical account of thought, i.e. of the meaningful sentence, is to be obtained through a philosophical account of language, i.e. of meaningful sentences. His concern was rather with the limits of what we can think, and he argued that those limits (which exclude the ineffable truths of metaphysics, ethics, aesthetics and religion) are to be uncovered by an investigation into the essence of symbolism. This investigation, he held, will also reveal what *cannot* be said in any possible language, but is inevitably and ineffably *shown* by any form of representation whatever. This Kantian preoccupation was shared neither by Frege nor by Russell. To the extent that Dummett's characterization of analytic philosophy fits the early Wittgenstein, to that extent it fails to fit either Frege or Russell. Furthermore, the later Wittgenstein repudiated this *Tractatus* doctrine. He did not think that investigating the use of the expression 'proposition' holds the key to the deepest, let alone to all the problems of philosophy. He repudiated his earlier view that there is such a thing as 'the general propositional form'. Indeed, he denied that the concept of a proposition holds any special foundational privileges relative to other philosophically problematic concepts. Philosophy has no foundations in an ineffable metaphysics of symbolism. An investigation of *thinking* is to be conducted by an examination of the use of the verb 'to think' and its cognates, and far from such an investigation exhausting the domain of analytic philosophy, it constitutes no more than a small part of the philosophy of psychology.

Dummett's characterization of analytic philosophy is historically unilluminating, and unhelpful in describing what is distinctive about the twentieth century revolution in philosophy. He claims that 'we may characterize analytical philosophy as that which follows Frege in accepting that the philosophy of language is the foundation for the rest of the subject'.[8] Not only is it debatable whether Frege would have accepted any such doctrine, it is certain that Moore and Russell alike would, indeed did, reject it.

---

[8] Dummett, 'Can Analytic Philosophy be Systematic and Ought It To Be?', p. 441.

Furthermore, the later Wittgenstein repudiated any such hierarchical conception of philosophy. No part of philosophy, in his view, is foundational relative to the rest. Philosophy is 'flat'. Finally, the most distinguished analytic philosophers of the post-war phase of analytic philosophy would not have accepted such a characterization of their conception of their subject. If Ryle's investigations into the concept of mind belong to analytic philosophical psychology, if von Wright's examination of the varieties of goodness belong to analytic axiology, if Hart's study of the concept of law belongs to analytic jurisprudence, if Dray's study of historical explanation belongs to the analytic philosophy of history, then little light is shed upon the character of analytic philosophy by characterizing it either as 'giving a philosophical account of thought by means of a philosophical account of language' or as holding that the philosophy of language is the foundation of the rest of the subject. Any characterization of 'analytic philosophy' which excludes Moore, Russell and the later Wittgenstein, as well as the leading figures of post-war analytic philosophy, must surely be rejected.

I shall take the term 'analytic' to mean what it appears to mean, namely the decomposition of something into its constituents. Chemical analysis displays the composition of chemical compounds out of their constituent chemical elements; micro-physical analysis penetrates to the sub-atomic composition of matter, disclosing the ultimate elements of which all substance is composed. Philosophical analysis harboured similar ambitions within the domain of ideas or concepts which are the concern of philosophy. Accordingly, I take the endeavours of the classical British empiricists to be a psychological form of analytic philosophy, for they sought to analyze what they thought of as complex ideas into their simple constituents. Such analyses, they believed, would not only clarify philosophically problematic notions, such as substance, causation, the self, etc., consigning some to oblivion and elucidating others, it would also illuminate the sources and extent of possible human knowledge.

I shall use the term 'twentieth century analytic philosophy' to characterize a dominant strand in twentieth century philosophy. It denotes a historical phenomenon, a distinctive movement in twentieth century thought. Like any historical movement, that movement underwent extensive change and development. I do not believe that it can be fruitfully characterized by reference to any single common tenet, or indeed by any conjunction of doctrines or methods accepted by all those who can with justice be called 'analytic philosophers'. Rather, it is to be understood dynamically. A variety of strands connect the thought of earlier phases of the movement with that of subsequent phases, even though no single strand of any moment runs through all phases. Nevertheless, I do not think it should be conceived to be a family resemblance concept. For that would detract from its usefulness as a historical category. Of course, this does not mean that twentieth century analytic philosophy had no precursors, both in the nineteenth century (among others Frege) and in earlier centuries (such as Aristotle, or Bentham), who shared *some* fundamental tenets and methodological principles with *some* phase or other of the modern movement.

Taking the term 'analysis' *au pied de la lettre*, twentieth century analytic philosophy is distinguished in its origins by its non-psychological orientation. One (Russellian) root of this new school might be denominated 'logico-analytic philosophy', in as much as its central tenet was that the new logic, introduced by Frege, Russell and Whitehead, provided an instrument for the *logical* analysis of objective phenomena. The other (Moorean) root might be termed 'conceptual analysis', in as much as it was concerned with the analysis of objective (mind independent) *concepts* rather than 'ideas' or 'impressions'. From these origins other varieties grew. Russell's Platonist pluralism, considerably influenced by the prewar impact of the young Wittgenstein, evolved into logical atomism. That in turn, fertilized by the *Tractatus* linguistic turn in philosophy (and greatly influenced by both Moore and Russell), gave rise to Cambridge analysis of the inter war years. At much the same time, the *Tractatus* was a major source of the different school of logical positivism, which arose in Vienna, was further fertilised by contact with Wittgenstein from 1927–36, and spread to Germany, Poland, Scandinavia, Britain and the USA. Both these phases of the analytic movement, in rather different ways, practised and developed forms of reductive and (its mirror image) constructive analysis. Under the influence of Wittgenstein in Cambridge and later of his posthumous publications, analytic philosophy entered yet another phase. Reductive and constructive analysis were repudiated. Connective analysis (exemplified in various forms in postwar Oxford) emerged, and with it therapeutic analysis. These different phases of the analytic movement overlapped temporally, and were mutually fructifying. Any detailed study of the movement must bear in mind that the development of analytic philosophy in this century was not linear, but has a complex synchronic, as well as diachronic, dimension.

In this lecture I shall try to give a synoptic view of the rise of analytic philosophy, to sketch its developments from its beginnings in Cambridge at the turn of the century, to its third great phase in the Vienna Circle prior to the second world war. Its final flowering in post-war Britain, in particular in Oxford, will not be discussed.

2. The first phase

Twentieth century analytic philosophy has its two-fold root in Cambridge at the turn of the century in the work of G. E. Moore and Bertrand Russell. Although it later merged with, it did not arise as a modern continuation of, the classical British empiricist tradition that runs from Hobbes and Locke to Mill. On the contrary, when Moore and Russell initiated their revolution in philosophy, the empiricist tradition in Britain was moribund. Since the 1860s Absolute Idealism had dominated philosophy in British universities, being a belated assimilation of Hegelian idealism tempered by British moderation. Kant and Hegel were thought to have dealt a death blow to empiricism. British philosophy seemed for awhile to be rejoining 'the main stream of European thought'[9], although, ironically, in Germany in mid-century Hegelianism was a spent force, and the neo-Kantians were triumphant.

The assault upon idealism arose both in Oxford, from Cook Wilson and his followers, and in Cambridge, where it was spearheaded by Moore, swiftly followed by Russell. Moore's revolt against idealism began with his 1898 Dissertation, and was rooted not in empiricism, let alone in common sense, but in Platonist realism. He insisted that relations are objective and mind-independent, and, with some qualifications, external. He rejected the monistic holism of Bradley's idealism, propounding instead an extreme form of pluralist, atomist realism.[10] The motivation was not unlike that which inspired Meinong and Brentano on the continent. In 'The nature of judgement' (1899), Moore defended the anti-idealist view that concepts are not abstractions from mind-dependent ideas, but are independent existences in their own right.

[9] Thus J. H. Muirhead, writing in 1924, in 'Past and Present in Contemporary Philosophy' in Muirhead ed. *Contemporary British Philosophy, First Series* (London: Allen and Unwin, 1924), p. 323. Muirhead's owl did indeed take flight after dusk.

[10] In a letter to Desmond MacCarthy, in August 1898, he wrote: 'I am pleased to believe that this is the most Platonic system of modern times.' (see T. Baldwin, *G. E. Moore* London and New York: Routledge, 1990), p. 40.

They combine to form propositions which are mind-independent objects of thought. Indeed, reality *consists* of concepts combined in propositions. The idealist notion that the unity of a proposition depends upon the synthesizing activity of consciousness was brushed aside in favour of unrestricted Platonism.[11] A true proposition does not *correspond* with reality, but *is* (a part of) reality. Contrary to the Absolute Idealist doctrine, the truth and falsehood of propositions are absolute, not a matter of degree. Truth is a simple, unanalyzable, intuitable property which some proposition; have and others lack.

Having repudiated the monism of the idealists, Moore turned, in his 1903 article 'The Refutation of Idealism', to assail the idea that reality is, in some metaphysical sense, subjective, spiritual or mental. This seminal article, rather curiously, took as its target not Bradleian metaphysics, but rather the Berkeleian claim that *esse* is *percipi*, although it is evident that Moore thought he had Kant too in his target area. His purpose was to sustain the claim that no good reason has been given for the doctrine that there is no distinction between experience and its objects, or that what we perceive does not exist independently of our perception of it. More generally, he insisted that objects of knowledge (including propositions), exist independently of being known. For knowing something, whether by way of perception or by way of thought, is quite distinct from the object of that knowledge; it is a cognitive relation *external* to the object of knowledge.

In these early papers, and in *Principia Ethica* (1903), Moore invoked 'analysis' – a method or approach to philosophy which was to have great influence over the next decades, despite the unclarity with which Moore explained what he meant by it. Sometimes, it seems, analysis is of properties or universals, sometimes of concepts, and sometimes of meanings of expressions. The difference is perhaps insignificant for Moore, since by and large he took a concept to be the meaning of an expression – what the expression 'stands for', and it was natural enough from this perspective to assimilate concepts to properties. What is clear is that analysis was not conceived to be of language, but of something objective which is signified by expressions. The analysis of the meaning of 'X' was variously specified as being: (i) the specification of the constituent

---

[11] He wrote to MacCarthy: 'I have arrived at a perfectly staggering doctrine ... An existent is nothing but a proposition: nothing *is* but concepts. There is my philosophy.' (see Baldwin, *op.cit.*, p. 41).

concepts into which the concept of X can be decomposed; (ii) the specification of what one sees before one's mind when one sees the meaning of X (i.e. the concept of X), e.g. a common property which may be simple and unanalyzable, or analyzable into constituents; (iii) the specification of how a given concept is related to and differentiated from other concepts. Far from intending to point philosophy in the direction of scrutiny of language and its use, Moore distinguished sharply between knowing the meaning of an expression, knowing its verbal definition and knowing its use on the one hand, and knowing the analysis of its meaning (or knowing the analysis of the concept expressed by a given verbal expression) on the other.[12] He differentiated knowing the meaning of an expression, construed as having the concept before one's mind, from being able to analyze that meaning, i.e. being able to say what its constituents are and how it is distinguished from other related concepts. One may know the meaning of an expression, but not know the analysis of the concept for which it stands. Moore conceived of analysing a concept as inspecting something which lies before the mind's eye, seeing the parts of which it is composed and how they are combined, and discerning how it is related to and distinguished from other concepts. Hence his theory of analysis implied that it is possible to analyze a concept without attending to its linguistic expression. In practice, however, as might be expected from his questionable conceptions of meaning and of concepts, his actual analyses, for example his (later) celebrated discussion of existence[13], were effected by comparing and contrasting the uses of expressions. The upshot of analysis was either the revelation that a given concept is simple and unanalyzable (as in the case of 'good'), or a specification of a set of concepts the combination of which was *equivalent* to the analysandum. The latter kind of case committed Moore to the linguistic representation of the analysis of complex concepts into their constituents by means of a paraphrastic equivalence, a conception which in practice converged on the general view of logico-linguistic analysis in the 1920s and '30s. However, in distinguishing one concept from another in terms of similarities and differences, he did not insist on finding equivalences. This approach became common in post second world war British philosophy, by which time Moore's conceptual realism had been

[12] See G. E. Moore, 'A Reply to my Critics', in P. A. Schilpp ed., *The Philosophy of G. E. Moore* (Evanston and Chicago: Northwestern University, 1942), pp. 660–7.
[13] G. E. Moore, 'Is Existence a Predicate', PASS XV (1936) 175–88.

rightly rejected. 'Conceptual analysis', as practised in Britain after the war, was an heir to Moorean analysis, in which the term 'analysis' was retained, but its implications of decomposition into simple constituents was jettisoned. Similarly, the term 'concept' was preserved, but its Moorean realist or Platonist connotations were abandoned. 'Conceptual analysis' thus conceived amounted, roughly speaking, to giving a description, for specific philosophical purposes, of the use of a linguistic expression and of its rule-governed connections with other expressions by way of implication, exclusion, presupposition, etc. (As Strawson has observed, the name 'connective analysis' (or 'elucidation') might have better conveyed this method of philosophy.) Though the expression 'analytic philosophy' continued to be widely used, its content had to a considerable degree lost contact with the philosophical perspective and aspirations in which it originated.

Just how far Moore's conception of philosophical method was from the linguistic orientation which analytic philosophy was subsequently to assume is evident from his later lecture 'What is Philosophy?', which he gave at Morley College, London, in 1910, and which is the opening chapter of his *Some Main Problems of Philosophy*. The most important objective of philosophy, Moore declared, is no less than

> To give a general description of the *whole* of the Universe, mentioning all the most important things which we *know* to be in it, considering how far it is likely that there are in it important kinds of things which we do not absolutely *know* to be in it, and also considering the most important ways in which these various kinds of things are related to one another. I will call this, for short, 'Giving a general description of the *whole* Universe', and hence will say that the first and most important problem of philosophy is: To give a general description of the *whole* Universe. (Ibid., pp. 1–2)

Such a description differs from physics in its generality. The very general *kinds* of things which Moore enumerates (starting from common sense beliefs) include the existence of material things and states of consciousness within a spatio-temporal framework. He further enumerates the various fundamental relationships in which things of these kinds stand to each other, e.g. the mind independence of material things, the spatial dependence of acts of consciousness on the location of the bodies whose states of consciousness they are. These metaphysical (or ontological) beliefs, which are, according to Moore, part of our Common Sense beliefs, have been controverted by many philosophical theories – particularly those of the Absolute Idealists against which Moore was campaigning, and it is part of the task of philosophy to investigate the truth of these beliefs and the ways in which we can establish them to be known with certainty to be true.[14]

Although Moore led the revolt against Absolute Idealism, Russell followed swiftly in his footsteps. Although taught by J. Ward, G. F. Stout and H. Sidgwick, it was McTaggart who influenced him most, and his first philosophy was idealist. His reaction against idealism started in 1898 under Moore's stimulus.[15] The philosophically most important feature of his youthful revolt was his rejection of Bradley's doctrine of relations as unreal and reducible to properties of their relata, with the consequence that reality cannot consist in a plurality of items externally related to each other in a multitude of ways. All relations were construed by Bradley as internal, i.e. as essential properties of their relata (although even as such they were held to be 'unreal'). Since everything is related to everything else, nothing short of the 'Absolute' comprises the truth as such. Russell saw what he called 'the axiom of internal relations' as informing five salient doctrines of Absolute Idealism: monism – the doctrine that there exists only one substance – the Absolute; the coherence theory of truth; the doctrine of concrete universals; the ideality or spirituality of the real; and the internal relation between the mind and the objects of knowledge. One of the many consequences of this strange doctrine is that it makes it impossible to give a coherent account of mathematical thought. For asymmetric relations essential to

[14] There is a striking resemblance between Moore's 'description of the most important things we know to be in the Universe' and Strawson's much later account of the basic particulars of any conceptual scheme which we can render intelligible to ourselves (see P. F. Strawson, *Individuals, an Essay in Descriptive Metaphysics* (London: Methuen, 1959). The equally striking differences are a measure of the transformation which analytic philosophy had undergone during the half century that separates the two books.

[15] He was later to write, 'I felt [the new philosophy] as a great liberation, as if I had escaped from a hot-house on to a wind-swept headland. I hated the stuffiness involved in supposing that space and time were only in my mind. I liked the starry heavens better than the moral law, and couldn't bear Kant's view that the one I liked best was only a subjective figment. In the first exuberance of liberation, I became a naive realist and rejoiced in the thought that grass is really green . . .' (Russell, *My Philosophical Development* (London: Allen and Unwin, 1959, p. 61). However, there was a difference between Russell's preoccupations and Moore's (ibid., p. 54). Moore's primary interest lay in the rejection of idealism, but, despite the above passionate reaction, Russell's was in the rejection of monism (although, as he pointed out, the two were closely connected through the doctrine of internal relations).

mathematics, such as 'is greater than' or 'is the successor of', are not reducible to properties of the relata without regress.[16] The proposition 'A is larger than B' is not reducible to 'There are magnitudes x and y, such that A is x and B is y' without the addition of 'and x is larger than y'. Recognition of external relations not only liberates philosophy of mathematics, it also abolishes the monism of the Absolute and admits that reality consists of a plurality of things.

Russell's adoption of analysis (as opposed to the neo-Hegelian synthesis associated with Absolute Idealism) had additional roots.[17] His reading of the works of Weierstrass, Dedekind and Cantor on the principles of mathematics coincided with his abandonment, under Moore's influence, of Idealism, and was a potent source of his conception of philosophical analysis. The work of the German mathematicians in analysing or defining mathematical concepts pertaining to the calculus, such as limit or continuity, 'swept away great quantities of metaphysical lumber that had obstructed the foundations of mathematics ever since the time of Leibniz'.[18] In particular, it liberated Russell from Kantian and Hegelian mis-construals of arithmetic and geometry, freeing his conception from any dependence upon *a priori* intuitions of space and time, and enabling him to repudiate the synthetic apriority of mathematical propositions.

Russell became persuaded that the royal road to truth in philosophy was analysis. He later wrote 'Ever since I abandoned the philosophy of Kant and Hegel, I have sought solutions of philosophical problems by means of analysis; and I remain firmly persuaded . . . that only by analysing is progress possible'.[19] Like Moore, Russell replaced Absolute Idealism not by empiricism, but

---

[16] Russell examined the matter in detail in chapter XXVI of his *The Principles of Mathematics* (London: Allen and Unwin, 1903). Subsequent references in the text to this work are abbreviated PrM.

[17] I am grateful to Ray Monk for pointing this out to me.

[18] See Russell, *Portraits from Memory and Other Essays* (London: Allen and Unwin, 1956), p. 24.

[19] Russell, *My Philosophical Development*, pp. 14f. In his preface to *Our Knowledge of the External World*, Russell generously characterizes the writings of Frege as 'the first complete example' of 'the logical analytic method of philosophy'. It is indeed true that Frege's philosophy of mathematics can be characterized as a complete example of the 'logical analytic method' *as Russell understood it in the second decade of the century*. However, Russell evolved his conception of analysis independently of Frege, and the application of the 'analytic method' to philosophy in general (in particular to epistemology, ontology, metaphysics and ethics), in *this* phase of the evolution of analytic philosophy was the work of Russell and Moore.

by unbridled Platonist realism. Initially, his conception of analysis was Moorean. In *The Principles of Mathematics* (written largely in 1900 and published in 1903), he wrote: 'All complexity is conceptual in the sense that it is due to a whole capable of logical analysis, but is real in the sense that it has no dependence upon the mind but only on the nature of the object. Where the mind can distinguish elements, there must *be* different elements to distinguish' (PrM 466). Analysis is essentially the decomposition of conceptually complex things (of which the world supposedly consists) into their simple unanalyzable constituents. When analysis terminates in simples or 'indefinables', the task of philosophy is

> the endeavour to see clearly, and to make others see clearly, the entities concerned, in order that the mind may have that kind of acquaintance with them which it has with redness or the taste of a pineapple. Where, as in the present case, the indefinables are obtained primarily as the necessary residue in the process of analysis, it is often easier to know that there must be such entities than actually to perceive them. (PrM p.xv)

Subsequent developments in his philosophy, however, enriched his conception of analysis, lending it a more pronounced logical-linguistic character, and giving it a reductive purpose.

In the *Principles*, inspired by Peano, Russell made his first attempt to carry out his logicist programme, attempting to show that arithmetic is reducible to purely logical notions alone.[20] Like Meinong, he accepted a referential conception of meaning, viz. that if an expression has a meaning, then there must be something which it means. As Meinong had argued, one must have due respect for what subsists without being actual. Accordingly, Russell held that every significant expression stands for something. His ontology included not only material particulars but also spatial points, instances of time, relations, universals, classes, correlates of vacuous definite descriptions such as 'the golden Mountain', logical objects for which logical expressions, such as 'or', were thought to stand, not to mention Homeric gods and chimeras.

Within a short time, however, what Russell later called his

---

[20] He later wrote 'The definition of number to which I was led . . . had been formulated by Frege sixteen years earlier, but I did not know this until a year or so after I had rediscovered it.' *My Philosophical Development*, p. 70). The *Principles* was originally intended to be the first volume of a two-volume work, the second of which was to be written in collaboration with Whitehead. As it turned out the second volume was never written, its place being taken by the far more sophisticated three-volume *Principia Mathematica*.

'robust sense of reality' reasserted itself. His Theory of Descriptions (1905) enabled him to reduce the luxuriant growth of subsistent entities which he had hitherto admitted. But there was a price for this achievement. It created the possibility of a rift between the grammatical structure of a sentence which expresses a proposition and the logical structure of the proposition expressed. Hitherto, Russell, like Moore, had taken for granted that the linguistic expression for a proposition is a transparent medium through which to view the real subject matter of philosophical reflection, namely propositions. For it was propositions, and not sentences, which, in his view, were the bearers of truth and falsehood, and he conceived of them, as did Moore, as mind-independent, non-linguistic objects, which contain not words but objective entities which he called 'terms' (which are akin to what Moore had called 'concepts'). The Theory of Descriptions, according to Russell, showed that the grammatical form of an expression (e.g. 'The King of France is bald', which has the subject/predicate form) may conceal the true 'logical form' of the proposition expressed. For the logical analysis of such propositions reveals the presence of quantifiers, identity, and logical constants. And 'denoting phrases', which seem to stand for something, do not do so at all, despite their occurrence as the grammatical subject of a sentence. This had far reaching implications for his conception of philosophical analysis.[21]

First, it transformed the previous conception of analysis from piecemeal analysis of the entities which are ostensibly mentioned by expressions in a sentence into a conception of analysis which recognizes the existence of what Russell called 'incomplete symbols' (of which definite descriptions are one kind). Such expressions occur in sentences, but have no meaning (do not stand for anything) on their own, although the sentence in which they occur does have a meaning, i.e. expresses a proposition. The analysis of such propositions is to be done by the transformation of the original sentence into a sentence from which the incomplete symbol has been eliminated. Consequently, secondly, analysis becomes an instrument for the uncovering of the true logical forms of propositions, which may be altogether different from the grammatical forms of sentences which express them. When Russell began to invoke facts, rather than propositions, as composing the world, he would express this by distinguishing the grammatical

---

[21] The matter is illuminatingly discussed in P. Hylton, *Russell, Idealism and the Emergence of Analytic Philosophy* (Oxford: Clarendon Press, 1990), chap. 6.

form of a sentence from the logical form of the fact. Indeed, he would argue that the primary task of philosophy is the investigation of the logical forms of the facts of the world. Thirdly, logic and its technical apparatus became the salient tool of analysis, enabling one to penetrate the misleading features of ordinary grammar and to gain insight into the true logico-metaphysical structure of things. Fourthly, the Theory of Descriptions forced Russell to concede greater importance to the investigation of language and symbolism than he had hitherto done, if only because it apparently revealed how misleading the symbolism of ordinary language is if taken to be a transparent medium through which to investigate the forms of propositions (or facts). Moreover, although Russell was loath to acknowledge it, the Theory of Descriptions exerted great pressure to consider analysis as an intralinguistic operation of sentential paraphrase for the purpose of philosophical clarification, and not a super-physical investigation into the logical structure of reality (either of facts or of propositions).

The Theory of Descriptions enabled Russell to pare down his ontological commitments. It strengthened his adherence to the principle of Ockham's Razor – that entities should not be multiplied beyond necessity. This set Russell on the high-road to reductive analysis in various forms, later articulated in 'the supreme maxim of all scientific philosophizing': *Wherever possible, logical constructions are to be substituted for inferred entities.* Analysis enabled one to show that apparent entities are actually merely logical constructions out of familiar items of which we have direct experience. Harnessed to Russell's distinction between knowledge by description and knowledge by acquaintance, it became an apparently powerful tool in epistemological as well as ontological investigations.

In 1901 Russell discovered the set-theoretic paradox, which so devastated Frege. In the course of his attempts to resolve it, he subsequently (1906) introduced the Theory of Types. By delimiting the range of significance (the range of possible values of the variable), i.e. the 'type', of a given propositional function 'x is F', one could exclude certain apparent (and paradox generating) propositions as meaningless. A function must always be of a higher type than its argument, hence while an individual (e.g. Leo) can be or not be a member of a class (of, say, lions), a class (such as the class of lions) can neither be nor fail to be a member of anything else but a class of classes. (So while it may or may not be true that Leo is a lion, it is neither true *nor false* that the class of lions is a lion

– it is quite meaningless.) Such restrictions are, Russell thought, rooted in the nature of things; a predicate cannot take itself as its argument because no property of objects can also be a property of properties. The Theory of Types distinguishes sharply between what is true or false on the one hand and what, although grammatically well-formed, is in fact meaningless. Again, while Russell originally conceived of entities, and not expressions, as being of one type or another, his theory was subsequently to be transformed and given a more markedly linguistic orientation by conceiving of type-distinctions as syntactical distinctions between kinds of expression.

Both Moore's and Russell's rather different styles of analysis inaugurated twentieth century analytic philosophy. Though both philosophers were adamant in their view that they were analysing phenomena, the foundations they laid were readily adjustable to logico-linguistic analysis once the 'linguistic turn' in philosophy had taken place.

3. The linguistic turn of the Tractatus

The expression 'the linguistic turn in philosophy' was introduced by Richard Rorty, who employed it as the title of an anthology of essays on philosophical method published in 1967.[22] The expression 'the linguistic turn' caught on and is indeed useful. I suggest that the linguistic turn in philosophy was begun, though not completed, by the *Tractatus*. This claim too is controversial, not only in respect of identifying what can rightly be denominated 'the linguistic turn', but also in ascribing its primary source to the *Tractatus*.

Anthony Kenny, following Dummett, has suggested that if analytic philosophy was born when the 'linguistic turn' was taken, 'its birthday must be dated to the publication of *The Foundations of Arithmetic* in 1884 when Frege decided that the way to investigate the nature of number was to analyse sentences in which numerals occurred'.[23] If the principle that the way to investigate the nature of X is to analyse sentences in which 'X' occurs signals the linguistic turn in philosophy, then the linguistic turn was already taken by

---

[22] R. Rorty, *The Linguistic Turn: Recent Essays in Philosophical Method* (Chicago and London: University of Chicago Press, 1967). Rorty attributes the phrase to Gustav Bergmann's *Logic and Reality* (1964).

[23] A. J. P. Kenny, *Frege* (Harmondsworth, Middlesex: Penguin Books, 1995), p. 211.

Bentham.[24] Although the context principle, whether in its Benthamite form or in its Fregean form, is of great importance, its introduction does not warrant the appellation 'the linguistic turn in philosophy'. And I doubt whether there is much to be gained by characterizing Bentham as the founding father of modern analytical philosophy, even though he explicitly engaged in what he called 'logical analysis'[25], and he is in various respects, one of the many precursors of twentieth century analytic philosophy.

It seems to me that in the course of the development of analytic philosophy in the early part of the century, there was a transformation that can justly be denominated 'the linguistic turn'. It is not a defining feature of analytic philosophy, for it postdates the

---

[24] Bentham propounded a form of context principle, closer to the later Wittgenstein than to Frege's (not altogether happy) contention that a word has a meaning only in the context of a sentence. He also advocated a method of analysis of those problematic terms which he called 'names of fictions' by means of sentential paraphrase. As Frege thought that the way to investigate the nature of number was to analyse sentences in which numerals occurred, so Bentham thought that the way to analyse the nature of duties, obligations and rights (as well as much else), was to analyse sentences in which the terms 'duty', 'obligation' or a 'right' occurred.

Bentham's form of context principle rightly stresses that the sentence is, as Wittgenstein was later to argue, the minimal move in a language game:

> But by anything less than an entire proposition, i.e. the import of an entire proposition, no communication can take place. In language, therefore, the *integer* to be looked for is an entire proposition – that which logicians mean by the term logical proposition. Of this integer, no one part of speech, not even that which is most significant, is anything more than a fragment; and, in this respect, in the many-worded appellative, *part of speech*, the word *part* is instructive. By it, an intimation to look out for the integer of which it is a part may be considered as conveyed. A word is to a *proposition* what a *letter* is to a word. (*Chrestomathia*, Appendix No. IX, 'Hints towards the Composition of an Elementary Treatise on Universal Grammar', in J. Bowring ed. *The Works of Jeremy Bentham* (Edinburgh: Tait, 1843), Vol. VIII, p. 188)

Like Frege, Bentham thought that certain kinds of names have a meaning, even though they do not stand for any idea. Unlike Frege, his interest was in names of what he called 'fictitious entities' (e.g. 'obligation', 'a right'), and his concern was not to show that they signify abstract entities, but rather that they have a meaning in a sentence even though they do not stand for anything at all. This is to be demonstrated by means of *paraphrasis*, i.e. 'that sort of exposition which may be afforded by transmuting into a proposition, having for its subject some real entity, a proposition which has not for its subject anything other than a fictitious entity' (*Essay on Logic*, in Bowring ed. *Works*, Vol. VIII, p. 246). Thus the term 'obligation' is to be explained by embedding it in a sentence ('phraseoplerosis'), and then 'exhibiting another [sentence] which shall present exactly the same import', but without containing the problematic expression in question. In the paraphrastic elimination of names of fictitious entities, it should not 'for a moment so much as be supposed that . . . the reality of the object is meant to be denied in any sense in which in ordinary language the reality of it is assumed' (*Chrestomathia*, Appendix No. IV, 'Essay on Nomenclature and Classification', section XX, in Bowring ed. *Works*, Vol. VIII, p. 126).

[25] Bentham, *Chrestomathia*, Appendix IV, 'Essay on Nomenclature and Classification', Section XIX, in Bowring ed. *Works*, Vol. VIII, p. 121.

Moorean and Russellian revolt against Absolute Idealism. But it is of the first importance, for it moulded the subsequent phases of the analytic movement. This transformation was effected by the *Tractatus*. I shall try to substantiate this claim by attempting an overview of some of the salient doctrines of the book.

According to the *Tractatus*, the function of language is to communicate thoughts by giving them perceptible form. The role of propositions is to describe states of affairs. Propositions are composed of expressions. Logical expressions apart, all expressions are either analyzable, or they are unanalyzable simple names. Simple names are representatives of objects in reality that are their meanings. Names link language to reality, pinning the network of language to the world. The elementary proposition is a concatenation of names in accord with logical syntax, which does not name anything, but says that things are thus and so. It represents the existence of a possible state of affairs that is isomorphic to it, given the method of projection. The logical syntax of any possible language mirrors the metaphysical structure of the world. Hence language is necessarily heteronomous, answerable to the logical structure of the world as a condition of sense.

Sentences are expressions of thoughts. Thought is itself a kind of language, composed of thought-constituents. The form of a thought, no less than of a sentence, must mirror the form of what it depicts. Language is necessary for the communication of thoughts, but not for thinking, which is effected in the language of thought. Mental processes of meaning and thinking inject content into the bare logico-syntactical forms of language. What pins a name to an entity in the world is an act of meaning *that* object by the name. What differentiates a mere concatenation of signs from the living expression of the thought is the employment of a method of projection, which is thinking the sense of the sentence, i.e. meaning, by the utterance of the sentence, *that* very state of affairs. So the intentionality of signs is parasitic upon the intrinsic intentionality of thinking and meaning. Understanding is a mental state or process that consists in interpreting the sounds heard and assigning them the same content as the speaker.

The salient achievement of the *Tractatus* was the positive account of the nature of the propositions of logic. The mark of propositions of logic is necessity. All necessity is logical. Logical propositions are tautologies, i.e. combinations of atomic propositions by means of truth-functional operations such that they are unconditionally true. All propositions of logic are senseless (all say the same, viz.

nothing). Every tautology is a form of a proof. So although they all say the same, different tautologies differ, inasmuch as they reveal different forms of proof. It is a mark of propositions of logic that in a suitable notation they can be recognized from the symbol alone. This reveals the nature of the propositions of logic and their categorial difference from empirical propositions. All the propositions of logic are given with the mere idea of the elementary proposition as such. For the logical connectives are reducible to the operation of joint negation, i.e. to conjunction and negation. Since it is of the essence of the proposition to be bipolar, and to be assertible, the notions of negation and conjunction are given by the mere fact that every proposition can be either true or false, and any pair of propositions can be conjunctively asserted. For 'It is false that p' is equivalent to 'Not-p', and the successive assertion of 'p' and 'q' is equivalent to the assertion of 'p & q'. Hence every possible truth-function of elementary propositions can be generated by the successive application of the operation of joint negation to elementary propositions. Tautologies and contradictions are the limiting cases of such combination.

This made it clear how misleading was the Frege/Russell axiomatization of logic, and their consequent appeal to self-evidence for their chosen axioms. For these axioms are not privileged by their special self-evidence. They are tautologies no less than the theorems. They are not essentially primitive, nor are the theorems essentially derived propositions, for all the propositions of logic are of equal status, viz. vacuous tautologies.

Equally revolutionary, and of paramount importance for the subsequent evolution of analytic philosophy, was the critique of metaphysics and the conception of future philosophy as analysis. Philosophy, according to the *Tractatus*, is categorially distinct from all sciences. Neither in its methods nor in its product is it akin to science. There are no hypotheses in philosophy. It does not describe the most general truths about the universe. Nor does it describe the workings of the mind. It does not investigate the metaphysical nature of things and describe them in synthetic a priori propositions, for there are none. There are no metaphysical truths that can be expressed in propositions. The only expressible necessity is logical. Hence all the propositions of the *Tractatus* are nonense, violations of the bounds of sense. The *Tractatus* is the swansong of metaphysics. Metaphysical truths are ineffable. But they are shown by ordinary propositions with a sense. Future philosophy will construct no theories, propound no doctrines, attain no knowledge. There are no philosophical propositions. The task of philosophy is the activity of logical clarification. Philosophy is not a cognitive discipline. Its contribution is not to human knowledge but to human understanding.

This non-cognitive conception of philosophy is unprecedented in the history of the subject. It marks a break with the first phase of analytic philosophy, and was to exercise great influence upon the Vienna Circle. It also paved the way for Wittgenstein's later conception of philosophy. All philosophy is a critique of language. Its task is to eliminate misunderstandings, resolve unclarities, and dissolve philosophical problems that arise out of the confusing surface features of natural language. This is to be done by analysis:

> The idea is to express in an appropriate symbolism what in ordinary language leads to endless misunderstandings. That is to say, where ordinary language disguises logical structure, where it allows the formation of pseudo-propositions, where it uses one term in an infinity of different meanings, we must replace it by a symbolism which gives a clear picture of the logical structure, excludes pseudo-propositions, and uses its terms unambiguously.[26]

The conception of analysis was *atomistic* and *logical*. Unlike Moorean analysis, it was *linguistic*: not an analysis of ideas, or of concepts (conceived as objective entities one can hold before the mind and inspect), but of propositions, i.e. sentences in their projective relation to the world. It would display the construction of propositions out of elementary proposition by means of truth operations. In addition to its task as clarifier of sense, philosophy has a more negative task, viz. to expose metaphysical statements as nonsense.

In six respects the *Tractatus* introduced the 'linguistic turn' in analytic philosophy, marking a break with Moore and Russell.

i) The aim of the book is to set the limits of thought. But it did so by setting the limits of language, i.e. by determining the bounds

---

[26] Wittgenstein, 'Some Remarks on Logical Form', *Proceedings of the Aristotelian Society*, suppl. vol. IX (1929), p. 163. Though written a decade later than the *Tractatus*, this essay (which Wittgenstein was later to reject as worthless) gives a perspicuous account of his earlier conception of analysis, and the only example of what he called 'the application of logic', with which he had not been concerned in the *Tractatus*.

between sense and nonsense. This put language, its forms and structure, in the centre of its philosophical investigation.

ii) The positive programme for future philosophy is the logico-linguistic analysis of propositions, i.e. of *sentences* with a sense.

iii) The negative task is the demonstration of the illegitimacy of metaphysical assertions. This was to be done by clarifying the way in which attempts to say something metaphysical traverse the bounds of language, endeavour to say something which by the intrinsic nature of *language* cannot be said.

iv) The key to Wittgenstein's endeavours lay in the clarification of the essential nature of the *propositional sign*. That was achieved by elucidating the general propositional form, i.e. by giving 'a description of the propositions of *any* sign-language *whatsoever* in such a way that every possible sense can be expressed by a symbol satisfying the description, and every symbol satisfying the description can express a sense, provided the meanings of names are suitably chosen.' (TLP 4.5)

v) The logical investigation of 'phenomena', the unfolding of their logical forms, is to be effected by the logical analysis of the linguistic descriptions of the phenomena. For the logical syntax of language is and must be isomorphic with the logical structure of reality.

vi) The greatest achievement of the book was the elucidation of logical truth. This was effected by an investigation of *symbolism*. The 'peculiar mark of logical propositions is that one can recognize that they are true from the symbol alone, and this fact contains in itself the whole philosophy of logic'. (TLP 6.113)

Although the *Tractatus* was rooted in a misconceived metaphysics of symbolism (e.g. that only simple names can represent simple things, that only relations can represent relations, that only facts can represent facts) it gave analytic philosophy a linguistic orientation it had not had before, and was far removed from the conceptions of philosophy and philosophical method of Frege, Moore and Russell.

4. Cambridge analysis and the Vienna Circle

The long term impact of the *Tractatus* was very far reaching, for the spirit of the *Tractatus* informs much contemporary philosophy of language. It is manifest in Chomskian conceptions of depth grammar, in the Davidsonian 'dream' of a theory 'that makes the transition from the ordinary idiom to canonical notation purely mechanical, and a canonical notation rich enough to capture, in its dull and explicit way, every difference and connection legitimately considered to be the business of a theory of meaning'.[27] It is exhibited in the fascination of linguists and theorists of meaning with the question of how it is possible to understand sentences we have never heard before and in the ways in which they attempt to answer this question,[28] and it lurks behind cognitive scientists' claims about the 'language of thought'. I shall not attempt to recount here how the ghost of the *Tractatus* still haunts contemporary thought, but merely dwell briefly upon its immediate impact on the next phases of analytic philosophy.

Its immediate impact was twofold. It was a major inspiration for Russell's logical atomism and for the emergence of Cambridge analysis in the 1920s. Its influence on Ramsey was great, and it was a primary inspiration for Wisdom's influential papers on logical constructions in 1931–3. It moulded Stebbing's conception of logical analysis, and was a guideline for the extensive debate in Britain in the 1930s about the nature of philosophy and of philosophical analysis – until Cambridge analysis was killed off by its begetter. The Cambridge analysts accepted the claim that the task of philosophy is not to add to human knowledge, but rather to elucidate the knowledge we already have by the logical analysis of sentences. Its purpose is to reveal the logical forms of facts, and, by reductive analysis, to show how logical constructions are generated out of the primitive constituents of experience. They eschewed traditional speculative metaphysics, and accepted the *Tractatus* conception of logic as consisting of vacuous tautologies.

The second sphere of the *Tractatus* influence was the Vienna Circle. Five major themes characterize the philosophy of logical positivism, and all were substantially influenced by the *Tractatus* and by contact with Wittgenstein between 1927 and 1936. It is striking that much of the influence involved extensive misreadings of its salient doctrines.

First, the logical positivists' conception of philosophy and of philosophical analysis was to a large extent the result of their reading of the book. They abandoned the logical atomism and the ontology of facts and their simple constituents. But they embraced

---

[27] D. Davidson, 'The Logical Form of Action Sentences' in N. Rescher ed., *The Logic of Decision and Action* (Pittsburgh: University of Pittsburgh Press, 1967), p. 115.

[28] For the reasons why this is a misbegotten question, see G. P. Baker and P. M. S. Hacker, *Language, Sense and Nonsense* (Oxford: Blackwell, 1984), chap. 9.

the idea that philosophy is not a cognitive discipline, that it is *toto caelo* distinct from science. The task of philosophy is logical analysis. Its positive use, according to Carnap, is to clarify meaningful concepts and propositions, and to lay the foundations for science and mathematics. Traditional philosophy is to be replaced by the investigation of the logical syntax of the language of science. Although this conception was derived from the *Tractatus*, it is noteworthy that Carnap's conception of logical syntax differs profoundly from Wittgenstein's, since he thought that different languages may have a quite different logical syntax, and that we are free to construct languages and their logical syntax as we please. Nevertheless, the Manifesto echoed the *Tractatus* in proclaiming that 'Clarification of the traditional philosophical problems leads us partly to unmask them as pseudo-problems, partly to transform them into empirical problems and thereby to subject them to the judgement of experimental science. The task of philosophical work lies in this clarification of problems and assertions, not in the propounding of special "philosophical" pronouncements.'

Secondly, the Circle advocated the demolition of metaphysics. Traditional metaphysical claims are to be exposed as nonsense. Pure reason alone can yield no knowledge. As they understood the *Tractatus*, it had shown that all reasoning is merely the tautological transformation of symbolism, and that metaphysical assertions are pseudo-propositions devoid of cognitive content. Unsurprisingly Wittgenstein was scornful of this aspect of the Circle's ideology, observing that there was nothing new about 'abolishing metaphysics'. What had seemed to him to be original in his anti-metaphysical remarks in the *Tractatus* was that by circumscribing the limits of language, he had made room for ineffable metaphysical truths, truths about the essential nature of the world, which cannot be expressed in a language, but which must inevitably be shown by the forms of any possible language. For this doctrine, the Circle justifiably had no sympathy.

Thirdly, the hallmark of logical positivism was the principle of verification, viz. that the meaning of a proposition is its method of verification. This was the basis for their criterion of meaningfulness. viz. verifiability. This criterion played a major role in the Circle's anti-metaphysical polemics, in contrast to Wittgenstein's strategy of arguing that there can be no expressible atomic necessary truths, and that any attempt to express such truths would involve illicitly employing a formal concept. The principle of verification was derived from conversations with Wittgenstein in 1929/30 and read back into the *Tractatus* by members of the Circle.[29]

Fourthly, the Circle aimed to uphold what they called 'consistent empiricism'. The major flaw in traditional empiricism was the difficulty in accounting for necessary truths. Of these, the propositions of logic and mathematics constituted the most formidable problem. As far as geometry was concerned, they tended to adopt Hilbert's view that pure geometry was a calculus of uninterpreted symbols and that applied geometry was an empirical theory of space. As far as arithmetic was concerned, they cleaved to logicism, thinking that the *Tractatus* had shown that arithmetical propositions are tautologies (whereas it had argued that they were pseudo-propositions). What seemed to them the greatest advance of the *Tractatus* was the claim that logical propositions are senseless tautologies, and that a priori reasoning is nothing but the tautological transformation of symbols. It had liberated the philosophy of logic from the incoherent idea that logical truth rests on an array of privileged self-evident axioms known by intuition. It also showed that contrary to Frege and Russell, there are no logical objects, and it rendered obsolete the idea that the propositions of logic consist of generalizations about logical entities, or forms, or the most general facts in the universe. As they understood Wittgenstein's account, he had shown that truths of logic are true in virtue of the meanings of the logical operators, hence a logical consequence of conventions of symbolism. Again, ironically, although the Circle's conventionalism was inspired by the *Tractatus*, and was rooted in Wittgenstein's explanation of the tautologous character of the propositions of logic, the conception of the Circle was far removed from his. Where they thought that the logical constants are arbitrary symbols introduced to form molecular propositions, he had argued that all of the logical constants are given together with the mere idea of the elementary proposition as such. Where they argued that logical propositions are consequences of conventions, he held that they are given by the essential nature of every possible language. In his view, they flow not from arbitrary conventions but from the essential bipolarity of the proposition, and they reflect the logical structure of the world. Logic, far from being determined by conventions, is transcendental.

The fifth plank in the logical positivists' platform was the

---

[29] See P. M. S. Hacker, *Insight and Illusion: Themes in the Philosophy of Wittgenstein* (Oxford: Clarendon Press, 1986), pp. 134–35.

programme of the unity of science. The idea has Cartesian ancestry, and was advocated in opposition to the view that there are different kinds of science with radically different methodologies and logical structures. In particular, they opposed the view that there is a sharp methodological and logical difference between the physical and the psychological, social and historical sciences. The thesis of the unity of science, at least in its original form, was committed to a reductionist programme of displaying all cognitively significant propositions as deducible from an array of basic propositions that constitute 'the given'. Although the *Tractatus* had not specifically discussed the thesis of the unity of science, it had argued that all propositions are reducible to an array of elementary propositions and their truth-functional combination. Non-extensional contexts were held to be reducible to extensional ones. On the plausible assumption that elementary propositions are verifiable in immediate experience, these claims provided a logical basis for the thesis of the unity of science.

It could readily be argued that of all the forms of twentieth century analytic philosophy, logical positivism has been the most influential, for not only was it the most vigorous, radical and influential movement in the interwar years, but, as a consequence of the fact that most members of the Circle fled to the USA, it was also destined to mould the shape of American post-war philosophy. However, in its 'classical' Viennese phase, it collapsed under both internal and external criticism. (i) The reductivist base was a bone of contention, opinion polarising between phenomenalism and physicalism. Despite extensive efforts, no one succeeded in producing a convincing reductive account of any general domain of discourse. (ii) The reductivism committed orthodox logical positivism to either methodological solipsism or to radical behaviourism. Neither proved acceptable. (iii) The thesis of extensionality proved exceedingly difficult to defend. (iv) Neither the principle of verification nor verifiability as a criterion of meaningfulness were capable of watertight formulation. (v) The conventionalism regarding necessary truth was shown to be inadequate. (vi) Substantial problems lay buried beneath the acceptance of classical logic as the basis for the logical analysis of language or for the rational reconstruction of the language of science. It is far from obvious that the logical operators of the calculus correctly represent the ordinary use of their natural language correlates. It is not evident that the latter are topic neutral. And it is evident that inference patterns licensed by the calculus do not exhaust the forms of licit inference we employ (e.g. determinate exclusion). (vii) The thesis of the unity of science came under attack from different directions. It is not obvious that there is 'only one science' or only one 'language of science' in Carnap's sense. Methodological monism came under increasing challenge from hermeneutics and from Wittgenstein's later philosophy. (viii) The conception of philosophy and of analysis was too narrow. If the whole of philosophy is characterized as the logical analysis of the language of science, this evidently precludes large areas of thought and discourse from the province of philosophy. Moral, legal and political discourse cannot be characterized as part of the language of science, nor can aesthetics. The superficiality of the logical positivists' brief forays into ethics was all too evident, and a reaction against their emotivism duly set in after the second world war. Legal and political philosophy slowly reasserted themselves.

Whether analysis is conceived as a matter of strict translation, or as a matter of the production of Carnapian reduction-statements, it proved to be far too restrictive for purposes of philosophical clarification. This became clear with the liberalisation of the notion of analysis that characterized the next phase in the evolution of analytic philosophy. The fountainhead of its final phase, characterized by connective and therapeutic analysis, was again Wittgenstein. Its waters flowed directly to Oxford, which, after Wittgenstein's retirement, became the leading centre of analytic philosophy for the third quarter of the twentieth century. Its manifold branches, and its remarkable and varied achievements are, however, a tale for another occasion.[30]

St John's College
Oxford OX1 3JD
England

---

[30] I have tried to tell this tale in *Wittgenstein's Place in Twentieth Century Analytic Philosophy* (Oxford: Blackwell, 1996).

WHY DID LANGUAGE MATTER TO ANALYTIC PHILOSOPHY?

John Skorupski

I. Introductory

Ideas about language and meaning have been at the heart of the analytic tradition. Taking the tradition as a whole, there has been no single idea. There were different ideas in Frege, in the Russell of logical atomism, in the Wittgenstein of the *Tractatus*. However the movement that developed from around the beginning of the 1930s did have a certain unity, which stemmed from the influence of a single dominant idea. The idea is that use exhausts meaning. It is not present in the earlier period and it is connected more clearly than were the ideas of the earlier period with a deflationary conception of philosophy – a conception according to which philosophical problems are pseudo-problems, problems to be dissolved not solved.

The conception of meaning as use and the deflationary view of philosophy grounded in that conception jointly define the analytic movement in what one might call its triumphalist phase. This linguistic turn occurred in Vienna. Frege and Russell gave it vital logical tools but not the philosophical vision in which meaning comes to be seen as use. Rules of language-use, in this vision, are the primitive data of philosophy – concepts and intentional mental states are to be explained by reference to them. The vision dominated the analytic movement both in its logical-empiricist phase – the empiricism of Vienna in the 30s – and in its phase of ordinary language philosophy in Oxford after the second world war.

Following Michael Dummett, I will refer to it as the 'priority thesis'.[1] I shall argue that it rests in part on an even more basic tenet – the notion that all cognitive content is factual content. And

---

[1] See Dummett, *Origins of Analytic Philosophy* (London: Duckworth, 1993), for a recent presentation of his view of the priority thesis, its origin and its role in the analytic tradition. My account of both its content and its historical origins is rather different. In taking 1930s Vienna to be the crucial turning point in conceptions of meaning and the a priori I agree with A. Coffa, *The Semantic Tradition from Kant to Carnap: To the Vienna Station* (Cambridge: Cambridge University Press, 1991).

I shall argue, relying on points which emerge from Wittgenstein's discussion of rule-following, that this more basic claim is incoherent. My conclusion will be that the priority thesis, and with it the conception of meaning as use, fails. Insofar as these theses are defining features of the 'analytical movement', we therefore ought to close that chapter in the story of twentieth century philosophy. This is not intended as a damning verdict on one of the most powerful forward steps in modern philosophy; important insights contained in the idea that 'meaning is use' survive, even if we treat them as insights about the normative nature of concepts rather than as insights about the form of language-rules. I would want to argue (though I shall not do so here) that these insights continue to vindicate the analytic movement's deflationary or dissolving view of metaphysics.

II. The Priority Thesis and the Conception of Meaning as Use

If meaning is use, to understand an expression or sentence is to master its use within a language. No more is required for full understanding than whatever is required for that. But why should we think that meaning is use? An essential premise underlying this view is that no language-independent account can be given of concepts and propositions. To talk of concepts or propositions is simply to talk indirectly of the use of expressions and sentences in languages – classes of same-use expressions and sentences. So grasping a concept is understanding (the use of) an expression in a language. Grasping a proposition is understanding (the use of) a sentence in a language. Attitudes to propositions and concepts are attitudes to sentences and expressions in a language. We cannot *explain* understanding an expression or sentence as knowing what concept or proposition it expresses – as though that concept or proposition were an entity independent of language, and 'understanding what concept or proposition is expressed' were a matter of knowing the correlation between the bits of language which do the expressing and the pre-existing non-linguistic item which is expressed.

This is the priority thesis. It need not deny that talk of concepts and propositions can be useful. Talking about them is a way of talking about language-understanding, without specifying the particular language. But we do not *explain* how a person understands the meaning of a word by saying that he or she possesses the concepts it expresses and knows that it expresses that concept. For possessing the concept just is knowing how to use the word (or some synonym) and that is what constitutes understanding it.

On the priority thesis, semantics and epistemology are one and the same. For the priority thesis says that there are no language-independent concepts constituted by their own language-independent epistemic norms. There are only rules of language. Epistemic norms, the subject-matter of epistemology, are simply rules of classes of language – the subject-matter of semantics. We are thus given an epistemic conception of meaning[2], or equivalently, a semantic conception of epistemology. Just one story now gives a unified account of the meaning and the epistemology of a language which we use. The traditional philosophical discipline of epistemology dissolves into the choice of a language and the setting out of the 'logical syntax' of that language.[3]

This view is central to logical empiricism. For logical empiricism held that there are only factual propositions – the province of science – and recommendations about how to speak or more generally, what to do. There are no non-factual propositions – and there are no factual propositions which lie beyond the province of science. Apart from facts there are only the rules which we adopt. In particular, a language is a set of recommendations, or rules. The rules stipulate when a sentence in the language is assertible.

But, to press a bit further, how exactly is the priority thesis connected to this conception of meaning and epistemology?

Consider the meta-linguistic proposition

(M) 'Ammonia smells' is true (in English) if and only if ammonia smells

If we know that (and know it solely by knowing the relevant semantic rules of English) then we know what proposition the English sentence 'Ammonia smells' expresses. But – as Michael Dummett has stressed – we can still ask what it *is* to know that 'Ammonia smells' is true (in English) if and only if ammonia smells.[4] There is a difference between knowing M and knowing

---

[2] 'Conception' in that it might not lead to a fully articulated theory of meaning – there is a big difference here between the Carnapian and the Wittgensteinian wings of the tradition. 'Epistemic' because the meaning rules it envisages state when assertion of a sentence and inference from it is warranted.

[3] What is abolished is the idea of epistemology as the study of norms of belief, understood as distinct from linguistic conventions or proposals. 'Epistemology' can still remain as the name for conceptual analysis of what kind of fact is asserted to hold when one says, for example, that a person *knows* that so-and-so is the case.

[4] 'What is a Theory of Meaning?', in Samuel Guttenplan, ed., *Mind and Language* (Oxford: Clarendon Press, 1975); reprinted in Dummett, *The Seas of Language* (Oxford: Oxford University Press, 1993) as 'What is a Theory of Meaning? (I)', with an appendix.

that the metalinguistic sentence which expresses it is true. I could know that this sentence in the meta-language (which in this case is itelf English) expresses a truth without knowing what the object-language sentence meant, because I could know it to be true in English without grasping the proposition it expresses.

Now according to the priority thesis to explain what it is to grasp a particular proposition is to give an account of what it is to understand some particular sentence or other. Suppose then that we try to combine the priority thesis with the claim that understanding 'Ammonia smells' is to be *explained* as consisting in a grasp of M. By the priority thesis, grasping M must in turn be explained as consisting in understanding some sentence. What sentence? Well, we could say that grasp of M is explained by giving an account of what it is to understand 'Ammonia smells' itself – but that would now put us in an explanatory circle. Apparently then we have to say that grasp of M is explained by giving an account of what it is to understand a sentence which expresses M. And then, by the same argument, we shall have to say that understanding that meta-linguistic sentence will in turn be explained as grasping the higher-level meta-linguistic proposition which specifies its truth-condition. Obviously this won't do. It cannot be the case that every language is understood only by prior understanding of a metalanguage in which biconditionals about truth-conditions of sentences in the language are expressed.

But the choice between a vicious circle and a vicious regress arises from the attempt to combine the priority thesis with the claim that understanding a sentence is to be *explained* as consisting in a grasp of a meta-linguistic proposition which specifies its truth-condition. Thus if we accept the priority thesis we must reject that claim.

Similar reasoning forces rejection of the claim that understanding a word is to be *explained* as consisting in a grasp of a meta-linguistic proposition – one which specifies its semantic value, or specifies the concept it expresses. We are lead to the conclusion that a conception of meaning must, in Dummett's words, be 'full-blooded' and not merely 'modest'. The point is that if we accept the priority thesis then we must reject the idea that understanding a word or a sentence can quite generally be explained as grasping a meta-linguistic proposition which exhibits its meaning by specifying its semantic value or its truth condition. On the contrary, we shall have to be able to say that grasping a meta-linguistic proposition of that kind can consist in understanding the word or sentence which it is about. For example, grasping M can consist – if one's home language is English – in understanding 'Ammonia smells': the very same understanding as is involved – in that case – in grasping the proposition *ammonia smells*.[5] Explaining what it is to possess a concept or grasp a proposition becomes a task for the theory of meaning, and not for some other branch of philosophy. Hence there must be a part of the theory of meaning which does more than simply stating what expressions of the language are true of and deriving from that truth-conditions for sentences of the language. There *may* be a truth-conditional part of this kind, but there must also be a part which goes beyond it. And this part will conform to the epistemic conception of meaning.

But if we take this part to consist in the specification of assertion conditions for sentences in the language, won't the argument we have just considered apply to it as well? Won't it equally show that understanding 'Ammonia smells' cannot consist in knowing the proposition that 'Ammonia smells' is assertible iff . . . ? The response is that knowing the assertion conditions of a sentence can consist in a practical ability to tell when it is right to utter it assertorically: a practical ability to recognise information states as warranting or not warranting that kind of utterance of the sentence. (We are talking here of a *normative* response: there is no attempt in this account of understanding to reduce or eliminate normative attitudes to language-use.) Precisely the same ability could of course be invoked to explain what it is to know the truth-conditions of a sentence. But that is the point. To respond in this way would concede that grasping truth-conditions is not something over and above, independent of, a practical grasp of use.

All of this has proceeded on the assumption that the priority thesis is correct. But why cannot we reject that thesis, and accept an account of concepts and propositions which is not language-relative?

The most significant approach of this kind is *Platonism*. I use the term to refer to the view that concepts and propositions are non-spatio-temporal entities known by non-perceptual intuition. Platonism, when combined with a truth-conditional view of meaning, may seem to offer an explanation of understanding. To

---

[5] This line of thought implies either (i) a 'deflationary', 'redundancy', or 'minimalist' theory of truth (a theory of the kind discussed e.g. in P. Horwich, *Truth* (Oxford: Basil Blackwell, 1990), or (ii) a verificationist theory of truth. So the disjunction of (i) and (ii) follows from the priority thesis.

know that 'straight' is true in English of straight things is to grasp, by non-perceptual intuition, the concept of straightness and to know that it is expressed by the English word 'straight'.

One can object, in this purported explanation of understanding, to the appeal to non-empirical intuition of concepts and propositions. But there is a different and clinching consideration – I will call it the 'no-intrinsic-meaning argument'. Wittgenstein uses it in various places, e.g. here:

> In attacking the formalist conception of arithmetic, Frege says more or less this: these petty explanations of the signs are idle once we *understand* the signs. Understanding would be something like seeing the picture from which all the rules followed, or a picture that makes them all clear. But Frege does not seem to see that such a picture would itself be another sign, or a calculus to explain the written one to us.[6]

Wittgenstein's point is that there is no such thing as an object which has intrinsic meaning, that is, which (a) has meaning irrespective of having that meaning conferred on it and (b) is such that perceiving or intuiting the object and knowing its meaning are one and the same. Even if we had access to objects in a Platonic third world, and had a mapping of terms and sentences onto these objects, that would do nothing for us unless those objects were already signs – signs which had intrinsic meaning. If their meaning were not intrinsic, the questions of what it is for them to have meaning and what it is for us to understand that meaning would again arise – even if we had an intelligible account of our acquaintance with them. The same would go for a picture in the world of physical representations or the world of mental representations. The objection does not have to do with the particular world we are talking about. It is not a merely naturalistic objection.

It certainly devastates the view that a person's understanding of language is to be explained in terms of his or her possession of concepts and propositions – *if possession of concepts and propositions is taken to consist of cognitive access to a class of objects*. So taken, concept-possession could not *in principle* have a justificatory or explanatory role. But we have not shown that the only alternative to a language-relative account of concept-possession is one which treats concepts

---

[6] L. Wittgenstein, *Philosophical Grammar*, edited by Rush Rhees, tr. by Anthony Kenny (Berkeley and Los Angeles: University of California Press), p. 40.

as intrinsically meaningful objects, mysteriously accessible to us. That would have to be shown, if we sought to derive the priority thesis from the no-intrinsic-meaning argument alone. Sometimes Wittgenstein seems to appeal to a dichotomy between an account of understanding which invokes access to intrinsically meaningful objects and one which invokes only grasp of language-rules:

> the mere fact that we have the expression 'the meaning' of a word is bound to lead us wrong: we are led to think that the rules are responsible to something not a rule, whereas they are responsible only to rules.[7]

The apparent suggestion here is that if we avoid reifying the meaning of a word into an intrinsically meaningful object then we have to accept that the rules governing its use constitute its meaning and are not 'responsible' to anything else. But may there not be a middle way – an account of concepts which neither reifies them nor makes them language-relative – and, given such an account, will it not be the case that a word which expresses a concept will have its meaning in the language set by rules which are 'responsible' to, or dovetail with, language-independent features of that concept?

An account fitting this description would be this: to grasp a concept is to acknowledge a pattern of epistemic norms. It is to be disposed to accept a particular pattern of thought-transitions as primitively justified. Epistemic norms, however, are not themselves rules of language. A theory of meaning for a language is not in the business of describing them – that is a matter for the theory of concepts (or epistemology). Thus the theory of meaning can describe the rules of the language truth-conditionally, and will dovetail with an account of concepts which is neither language-relative nor Platonistic, but characterises possessing concepts as acknowledging patterns of epistemic norms.

Such an approach rejects the priority thesis, but still accepts the no-intrinsic-meaning argument against Platonism. It provides, one might say, a full-blooded theory of concepts and a modest theory of meaning. So the question arises whether there is a case for the priority thesis which is independent of the no-intrinsic-meaning argument.

---

[7] Reported in G. E. Moore, 'Wittgenstein's Lectures in 1930–33', in Moore, *Philosophical Papers* (London: George Allen and Unwin, 1959), p. 258.

III. Facts and Norms

By analogy to the slogan that meaning is use, one might say that concepts are cognitive roles. The no-intrinsic-meaning argument does not decide the choice between the two slogans.

Are the slogans complementary, or does one make the other redundant? It is a question of the difference between norms and language-rules. By a 'norm' I mean a true normative proposition about reasons. An *epistemic* norm is about reasons to believe – about the relation '. . . gives *x* reason to believe that *p*'. So the slogan 'Concepts are cognitive roles' says that to possess a concept is to acknowledge a pattern of epistemic norms. In contrast, a rule is not a *proposition* at all. It cannot be said to be true or false. It is the content of an explicit stipulation or implicit convention. The priority thesis comes down to saying that we cannot treat purported epistemic norms as ultimately distinct from rules of a language. Talk of norms constituting a concept must reduce to talk of language-rules constituting the meanings of words.

The no-intrinsic-meaning argument does not establish this thesis. We must look elsewhere – to an extraordinarily influential assumption which is made both by the Platonist *and* by Viennese logical empiricism, Oxford ordinary-language philosophy, and Quinean naturalism. The assumption is that all propositions are factual. Assertoric and judgeable content is factual content.[8] In that case, if there are normative propositions there must be a domain of 'normative facts'. Well, we do talk about 'the fact that' one ought to come to the assistance of distressed people, or 'the fact that' one ought to accept the simplest explanation of the data. But we are not, I think, indulging in ontology. There is indeed a substantial, ontologically committing, use of the word 'fact': in this use of the word, the idea of 'normative fact' seems to be a kind of category mistake. The stubborn thought that makes it seem a category mistake is a cousin, one might say, of the no-intrinsic-meaning argument. It is the thought that no fact, in any world (natural or non-natural), is intrinsically normative. Acknowledging a norm cannot *consist* in recognising a fact. Norms are no more facts than meanings are things. And it is in this ontologically committing

---

[8] 'what else but a fact can a statement express? In what sense could something be called "true" or "false" if it does not designate an existing or nonexisting fact?' R. Carnap, 'Pseudo-Problems in Philosophy: the Heteropsychological and the Realism Controversy', in R. Carnap, *The Logical Structure of the World*, tr. by E. A. George (London: Routledge and Kegan Paul, 1967), p. 341.

sense of 'fact' that the claim that all propositions are factual is to be understood.

If all propositions are factual and there are no normative facts, normative utterances, such as 'You have reason to come to the assistance of distressed people', or 'You have reason to accept the simplest explanation of the data' cannot be assertions but must rather be understood as recommendations, proposals, prescriptions and so forth. In particular, then, it can become plausible to hold that the alleged epistemic norms which constitute concepts should really be seen as prescriptions as to the use of words. But this conclusion is not enforced by the powerful double-barrelled weapon that says no object is intrinsically meaningful and no fact intrinsically normative. It requires the further claim that all assertoric content is factual. Only then do we get the dichotomy of facts and rules which generates the priority thesis.

Although Wittgenstein often seems to assume the dichotomy (as in the passage quoted above), it is also true that Wittgenstein's later thinking drives a wedge through it. I have in mind his reflections on what it is to follow a rule. He highlights the point that to apply a rule is to exercise normative judgement. What view he takes of it, having highlighted it, is a matter of dispute. But suppose we assume, contrary to some readings of his philosophy of language, that he does not intend to *deny* that the question 'Has the rule been applied correctly?' can have a true answer. His view is neither the nihilist one that there is no true answer, nor the radical-conventionalist and expressivist one that the answer in every case expresses a decision. He accepts that it can be determinately true that if you're following the rules of English you ought to call this patch here 'yellow' (though there can also be vague or indeterminate cases). I also assume – contrary, admittedly, to much current discussion – that Wittgenstein was not a reductionist. It was not his view that 'If you're following the rules of English you ought to call this patch here "yellow"' has a non-normative truth-condition, consisting say in a fact about the speech-dispositions or mental states of certain language-users. But if nihilism, radical conventionalism and reductionism are all false, then we have here an example of a determinately true normative judgement which corresponds to no fact (in the ontologically committing sense)'.[9]

----

[9] It does not correspond to the fact that the patch *is* yellow. Rather, the English sentence 'The patch is yellow' can express a fact because the normative proposition 'If you're following the rules of English you ought to call this patch "yellow" ' can be determinately true.

The upshot is that a thinker who follows rules must grasp norms *as well as* facts and rules. Commitment to the existence of norms is entailed by our very description of an entity as a rule-follower – if there are rules the dichotomy of facts and rules is not exhaustive.

Applying a rule involves a spontaneous or autonomous normative capacity which is reducible neither to judgements about what is the case nor to familiarity with conventions or stipulations. But why should interpretative normative judgements, judgements about the right way to apply a rule to a case, be the *only* instances of true normative propositions? We naturally and stably converge on many primitive judgements about what there is reason to think, feel, or do. Spontaneity and stability of normative judgement is present in all these cases. They are genuine judgements; no more is needed to show they have genuine propositional content.

Now we can formulate a real contrast between an epistemic conception of meaning and an epistemic conception of content (or concepts). Both hold that a truth-conditional theory of meaning must be supplemented if one wants a full account of language-understanding. But the epistemic conception of meaning takes it that an account of the cognitive roles of concepts reduces to an account of rules for use of expressions in a language. It holds that the required supplement is still *semantic*. On this view, there is a level of semantic theory which describes conventions for introducing and eliminating terms in a language. Conventions stipulating when a sentence is assertible and what is inferable from it are determined by them. They constitute the language, and the level of semantic theory at which they are stated – call it 'the cognitive-role level' – is more fundamental than the truth-conditional level. In contrast, an epistemic conception of content takes the objectivity of norms seriously, and holds that an account of concepts can consist in an account of the epistemic norms regulating their introduction and elimination in one's thinking. Such an account is not a level of semantic theory, for it does not purport to describe rules of a language. The conception denies the identity of semantics and epistemology. As far as the semantics of a language is concerned, it can hold that the truth-conditional account is fully adequate.

But we have still to consider a very important and attractive corollary of the epistemic conception of meaning. The corollary is an account of how a priori knowledge derives from a grasp of meaning, and it is one of the most potent arguments in the epistemic conception's favour – one might say it is *the* reason why language mattered to analytic philosophy.

IV. A Prioricity and Normativity

An epistemic conception of meaning greatly enlarges the empiricist idea that aprioricity is analyticity – that an a priori warrant for an assertion is one obtainable from a grasp of its meaning alone. Because it introduces rules of language at the cognitive-role level, it is able to give a new account of analyticity which differs from what one might call the Kant/Mill account.

In this account a class of sentences is identified as uncontroversially empty of content, or a class of inferences as uncontroversially 'merely apparent', and then these, together with sentences or inferences reducible to them by explicit definitions, are defined as analytically true. Take for example 'Anyone who is a father is a parent' or 'He's a father. Therefore he's a parent'. The explicit definition is ' "x is a father" $=$ Df "x is male and x is a parent"'. The contentless sentence might be 'A father is a father' and the inferences acknowledged as merely apparent would in this case include and-elimination. But as Mill particularly emphasized, this account of analyticity does not guarantee that *all* logic is analytic. It is not uncontroversial that all logically valid inferences are merely apparent, even if it is uncontroversial that and-elimination is. (If even this is rejected the class of analytic truths is even smaller: e.g. 'Tomorrow is the day after today'.) In this respect, the Kant/Mill account contrasts with the 'Kant/Frege' account, which characterises analyticity outright as derivability, with explicit definitions, from logic. However, the Kant/Frege account does not (in Frege's case at least) claim that analyticity is truth by virtue of meaning alone or that analytic propositions are empty of content – even though it holds that analytic truths are a priori. It is therefore unacceptable to a clear-headed empiricist.

In contrast to both of these approaches the new account of the a priori provided in Vienna in the 1930s *does* simultaneously claim that all logic is analytic and that analyticity is truth by virtue of meaning alone. It promises an empiricist account of the aprioricity of logic and mathematics.[10]

In the new account, as in the Kant/Mill account, a sentence is analytic when a justification for asserting it can be derived

[10] For further discussion of these matters see Coffa, *op.cit.*, and Skorupski, *English-Language Philosophy 1750–1945* (Oxford: Oxford University Press, 1993), and 'Empiricism: British and Viennese', in Jaakko Hintikka & Klaus Puhl, eds. *The British Tradition in 20th Century Philosophy, Proceedings of the 17th International Wittgenstein-Symposium*, (Vienna: Hölder-Pichler-Tempsky, 1995), pp. 285–299.

exclusively from a grasp of its meaning. But the rules which constitute that meaning will now include introduction and elimination rules statable only at the cognitive-role level. An example will explain what I mean. Consider the following introduction rule for the English word 'yellow':

> (1) The occurrence of a visual experience as of a yellow object in one's visual field warrants, in the absence of defeating information, assertion of the sentence in English 'There's something yellow there'.[11]

This is a rule formulated at the cognitive-role level. In contrast, if (as is plausible) 'yellow' is semantically simple then a truth-conditional semantics for English will contain only the following dictionary rule:

> (2) 'yellow' is true (in English) of x if and only if x is yellow.

Consider now the following normative proposition:

> (3) The occurrence of a visual experience as of a yellow object in one's field of vision justifies, in the absence of defeating information, a judgement that there's something yellow there.

This is not a meta-linguistic statement of a rule of English as (1) is. It is a normative proposition stated in English. What is the relation between them? Given the priority thesis, (3) must be in some way an expression of (1) or an equivalent to (1) alone. It cannot be a genuine normative proposition. Rather, sentence (3) is 'assertible a priori' in English because its warrant derives solely from a rule of the language – for English the rule will be (1), while for other languages which have a sentence synonymous to (3) it will be a rule equivalent to (1). Let us allow, for the sake of argument, that the details of this can be filled in coherently. However it is done, the crucial point is that it provides an explanation of how a priori knowledge of (3) is possible, in a way that no appeal to (2) could do. I have a priori knowledge of (3) in virtue of grasping rule (1), or some analogous rule in another language.

In short, the priority thesis generates a new account of aprioricity as analyticity because it produces a conception of

---

[11] As I have formulated (1), the relation *warrants assertion of* holds between a state of visual experience – something which is not a sentence – and a sentence. Some philosophers (including some members of the Vienna Circle) have found this unacceptable. But if a language has empirical content at all it must contain rules linking the assertibility of certain sentences in the language to the language-user's experience and memory.

meaning as use, a conception which postulates introduction and elimination rules at the cognitive-role level. Indisputably, this is important and new – a major twentieth-century contribution to philosophy. But is it right? *Does* the aprioricity of (3) depend in any way on there being a rule of English expressible by (1), or some analogous rule for another language? Well, it's far from obvious that it does depend on that. Do we want to say that (3) is 'a priori'? What makes us want to say it is, if we do, does not seem to stem from the fact that some language, English or another, contains some rule. Rather, the essential point is simply that we converge, on critical reflection, in finding (3) primitively or spontaneously compelling. It is a fundamental epistemic norm: it expresses a primitive normative response. Acknowledging it does not consist in learning any linguistic convention or stipulation. It's the other way round: training in linguistic conventions *assumes* such primitive normative responses. In teaching (2) we assume the existence of belief-forming dispositions responsive to (3). And once a person has learned (2), he or she will see the truth of (1), understood now not as a language rule but as a consequence of (2) and (3).

On the other hand, we have accepted the point that no fact is intrinsically normative. So acknowledging (3) does not consist in knowledge of any fact, natural or non-natural. What then, is its epistemology? As for any other fundamental norm, be it of belief, action or feeling, it is the dialogical epistemology of reflective examination and critical convergence. That is the epistemology characteristic of the normative: it is not the epistemology appropriate to propositions which depict the existence of a state of affairs.

Much more needs to be said – needless to say! – about the epistemology of the normative before we can fully secure the essential point here, viz. that there can and must be normative as well as factual judgeable contents. That is not a task for this paper. For present purposes it is enough to pin down how the view that concepts are patterns of epistemic norms differs from the view that they are patterns of language-rules. The former view requires us to acknowledge that the normative and the factual are both domains of judgement, consisting of propositions with truth-value. If this is defensible, then we can say that (3) expresses a norm partially constitutive of the concept *yellow*. We *can* also say it is a 'conceptual truth'. At any rate it is concept-constituting and it is true. *But its status as a conceptual truth in this sense in no way explains how it might be 'a priori'.* The way it is known to be true is the way that any fundamental norm is known to be true; its epistemology is that appropriate to fundamental norms in general. It is not *because* it is a 'conceptual truth', constitutive of the concept *yellow*, that it is true. No matter. If concepts are constituted by norms of reasoning, and if we can get a satisfactory account of normative knowledge, we do not *also* need a substantive theory of 'a priori' which goes beyond Kant/Mill analyticity. An account of normative knowledge will do what an account of the a priori was meant to do.

I assumed earlier that Wittgenstein is neither a nihilist nor a radical conventionalist nor a reductionist about rule-following. If all this is right then the later Wittgenstein needs a distinction between rules and norms of the kind made here. His own reflections on rule-following show that to avoid this trilemma one must repudiate the Viennese dichotomy of facts and rules. For that dichotomy, when joined to the points that no object has intrinsic meaning and no fact is intrinsically normative, produces the priority thesis, the linguistic theory of the a priori and radical conventionalism about logic and rule-following.

But did Wittgenstein go beyond the dichotomy? Reading his later writings on 'grammar' and 'rules' with this question in mind it is hard to come up with an answer. Michael Dummett reads Wittgenstein as a radical conventionalist. Others disagree.[12] But they tend to reflect Wittgenstein's own murkiness. In a valuable discussion of Wittgenstein's notion of a criterion, for example, Peter Hacker comments thus:

> To say that q is a criterion for W is to give a partial explanation of the meaning of 'W', and in that sense to give a rule for its correct use. The fact that the critical relation between q and W may be neither arbitrary (in one sense at least) nor stipulated, that in innumerable cases we could not resolve to abandon the normative relationship without a change in our form of life, and in many cases could not abandon it all, does not imply that it is empirical, let alone that it is a matter of *Wesensschau*. We may concede that certain concepts are deeply embedded in our lives, occupy a pivotal role in our thought and experience, yet still insist that their use is rule-governed, a matter of *nomos* rather than *phusis*.[13]

[12] Cp. M. Dummett, 'Wittgenstein's Philosophy of Mathematics', *Philosophical Review*, vol. 68 (1959) and 'Wittgenstein on Necessity: Some Reflections', in Dummett, *The Seas of Language*, op. cit, with B. Stroud, 'Wittgenstein and Logical Necessity', *Philosophical Review*, vol. 74 (1965).

[13] *P. M. S. Hacker, Wittgenstein, Meaning and Mind, An Analytical Commentary on the Philosophical Investigations*, vol. 3 (Oxford: Basic Blackwell, 1995), p. 552.

Note how the line of thought here goes from acknowledging that the relationship is 'normative' to the conclusion that – however inescapable for us, however felt as a constraint rather than as a stipulation – it must yet be a 'rule', a matter of convention rather than nature.

But why cannot it be acknowledged that it is normative without being in *any* sense a convention? It is hard to see what could be at work here other than the philosophical thesis that all propositions, judgeable contents, are factual. Perhaps it is impossible to tell how far Wittgenstein thought his way past this thesis. On the one hand he was not (in his later thought) burdened by the realist semantic assumptions about truth and reference which lead to it. But on the other hand his constant insistence that 'training' determines the 'logical grammar', or framework, of our language-games at least suggests that he did not repudiate the thesis. For one is 'trained' to observe rules: the process of acknowledgeing a norm – spontaneously, autonomously – is a process of *education* not 'training'. To see clearly that the normative is in this fashion a domain of the understanding, something we judge of, one must decisively dislodge the Viennese dichotomy of facts and decisions – the most fundamental dichotomy, one might say, of modernism in the analytic mode.

Norms are indeed like rules in this respect: we do not find them in the world. They are presupposed in cognition of a world. That view still has certain strong affinities with Wittgenstein's later philosophy, even if it is not his. To adopt it is to give up the analytic movement's cardinal notion that *language-use* is the primitive phenomenon for philosophy. But it may still preserve its deflationary view of metaphysics. The notion that metaphysical problems are pseudo-problems, to be dissolved not solved, remains a very important and controversial philosophical idea. In the end, of course, the question is not who thought it but whether it is true and if so how.[14]

Department of Moral Philosophy
University of St. Andrews
St. Andrews KY16 9AL
Scotland

[14] This article is drawn, with revisions, from sections of a longer discussion in Skorupski 'Meaning, Use, Verification', in Bob Hale and Crispin Wright, eds. *The Blackwell Companion to the Philosophy of Language*. Oxford: Basil Blackwell (forthcoming).

INDEX

analysis, 36, 41–7, 50, 55–6, 58–66, 70, 72–6
  conceptual/linguistic, 3–4, 8, 60, 65
  atomistic vs. reductive vs. connective, 56–7, 60, 70, 72
analytic philosophy
  definition of, vii–xiv, 3–9, 15–16, 17–19, 35–41, 50, 51–60, 60, 77, 91
  logical vs. ordinary language, 1, 5, 56
analytic/synthetic, 26, 29, 74, 87–90
a priori *see* analytic/synthetic
Aquinas, T., 11, 14, 52
argument and justification, 7–17
Aristotle, 11, 14, 52
Austin, J. L., 1, 18, 52

Bentham, J., 67
Bergmann, G., 18
Bergmann, J., 24
Berkeley, G., 43
Black, M., 18
Bolzano, B., ix, 1, 6, 11
Borges, L., 2
Bradley, F. H., 52, 57, 61
Braithwaite, R., 38
Brentano, F., 57

Cambridge analysis, 51, 71–2
Cantor, G., xi, 41, 43–4, 62
Carnap, R., x, 6, 17, 18, 19, 32, 73, 76
categories, 33–4
Chomsky, N., 71
Church, A., 18
concept, 57–60, 82–6
context-principle, 35–6, 66–7

Davidson, D., 13–14, 71
Dedekind, R., xi, 41, 46, 62
Derrida, J., 12, 14
Descartes, R., 14

Dilthey, W., 4
Dray, W., 55
Dummett, M., vii–ix, xi–xii, 6, 18, 19, 35–41, 47, 50, 52–4, 66, 77, 90

empiricism, vii, 20–1, 55, 57, 74
Erdmann, B., 21
ethics, 15–16
Evans, G., viii, 36–7

Føllesdal, D., ix
Frege, G., vii, ix–x, xii, 1, 5, 6, 9, 12, 17–34, 35–6, 41, 48–9, 51, 52–4, 66–7, 69, 74, 77, 82, 87

Gauss, K. F., 21
Geach, P., 18
Goodman, N., 10–11

Hacker, P. M. S., xi–xii, 90–1
Harkness, J., 45
Hart, H. L. A., viii, 55
Hegel, G. W. F., 11, 41–7, 52, 57, 62
Heidegger, M., viii, 12, 52
von Helmhotz, H., 21
hermeneutics, viii–ix, 1, 4, 13–14
Hobbes, T., 57
Husserl, E., vii–viii, 6, 11, 12, 17

identity statement, 25–6, 28–9

Joachim, H., 40
judgment, 23–6, 49–50
  see also proposition

Kaila, E., 6
Kant, I., 11, 20, 23–6, 52, 54, 57, 58, 62, 87, 90
  see also Neo-Kantianism
Kenny, A., 66

language *see* linguistic turn, meaning, semantics
Leibniz, G. W., vii, 6, 21–2, 44
Liebig, J., 21
linguistic turn, 35–6, 39–40, 52–4, 66–71; *see also* priority thesis
Locke, J., 57
logic, 21–9, 38–40, 51, 68–71, 74
logical positivism *see* Vienna Circle
Lotze, H., 24, 29–30

Marxism, viii–ix, 1, 4, 15
Mach, E., 8
mathematics, 19–22, 26–33, 41–6, 6
McGinn, C., viii
McTaggart, J. E., 42, 61
meaning, 29, 33–4, 37–8, 48–9, 58–9
  and use, 60, 76–83
  see also semantics, sense/reference, linguistic turn
Meinong, A., 57, 63
Mill, J. S., 20–1, 87, 90
Monk, R., x–xi
Moore, G. E., vii, viii, xii, 1, 3, 5, 6, 8, 9, 19, 41, 44, 45, 47–8, 54–61, 64, 66, 70
Morley, F., 45

Nagel, T., viii
naturalism, 13–14, 82, 84
Neurath, O., 19
Neo-Kantianism, ix, x, 1, 4, 23–6, 29–32, 57
norms, 81–91
Nietzsche, F., 52

Occam's razor, 65
Oxford philosophy, 51, 76, 84

Pascale, P., 52
Peano, G., viii, 63
Peacocke, C., viii, 37
phenomenology, ix, 1, 4, 12
Popper, K., viii
proposition, 37–8, 47–9

psychologism, xii, xiii, 35–40, 56
priority thesis, 77–91

Quine, W. V., 3, 7, 8, 13–14, 84

Ramsey, F. P., 72
Rawls, J., ix, 7, 10–11
Rickert, H., 30–1
Rorty, R., 66
Russell, A., 44
Russell, B., vii, viii, x–xi, 1, 5, 6, 8, 9–10, 12, 17, 19, 32, 33, 35–50, 51, 54–7
  theory of descriptions, 64–5
Ryle, G., 52, 55

Scheffler, I., 10–11
Schlick, M., 8, 9, 19
Scholz, H., 6
science, 75–6
Searle, J., viii, 12
Sellars, W., 13–14
semantics, 18, 21–3, 29–34, 35, 36, 79–80
sense/reference, 29–30, 48
Sidgwick, H., 61
Sigwart, C., 24
Skorupski, J., xii–xiii
Stebbing, S., 72
Stegmüller, W., 13
Stout, G. F., 61
Strawson, P. F., 52, 60

tautologies, 68–9, 72, 74
Thales, 37
Trendelenburg, A., 22
truth, 8, 22, 29–31, 34

Urmson, J. O., 9

Vienna Circle, vii, 51, 56, 70, 72–6, 77, 84, 87, 91

Waismann, F., 3, 8, 9
Ward, J., 61
Wedberg, A., 6

Weierstrass, K., xi, 41, 45, 62
Whitehead, A. N., 46, 51
Wilson, C., 57
Windelband, W., 24, 29–31
Wittgenstein, L., vii, ix, xi, xii, xiii,
    1, 8, 9–10, 17, 18, 19, 32, 33, 36,
    39–40, 41, 49–50, 51, 52–55,
    66–76, 77, 82, 85, 90–1
Wisdom, J., 72
von Wright, G. H., 9, 13

Zeno, 43